Bianca Zapatka

VEGAN
& Easy

70 amazingly simple and delicious recipes

lotus
publishing

Chichester, England

Introduction

If you enjoyed my first best-seller *Vegan Food Porn* and simply can't get enough of the recipes, then I know you'll love the delicious recipes in this book too! *Vegan Food Porn* contains a shopping list for all the basic ingredients for vegan cooking. But don't worry if you don't have a copy; you can simply use the ingredients lists for each of the recipes.

Ready? Then let's go!

What do I mean by 'easy'?

As with so many things in life, 'easy' means different things to different people. When it comes to recipes, some people consider easy to mean something that can be made really quickly. Others think easy recipes are those with a simple method that take just a few steps to prepare. And then there are others who find recipes easy if they require only a few ingredients, saving the hassle of an enormously long shopping list.

Practice makes perfect

For me personally, the recipes I find easy are the ones I've practiced a lot. We all know practice makes perfect – and it's no different when it comes to cooking and baking. So why not try something new? I'm sure you'll find these recipes just as easy as I do!

Easy to make at home

If you've been following me on Instagram or you subscribe to my blog, you'll already know that I like to make pretty much everything myself. Whether it's gnocchi, pasta or pizza dough – everything tastes better when it's homemade! It's also a good way to save money and know exactly what's in your food. Plus, once you've established a routine, 'homemade' can be really easy too!

In a hurry? No problem!

The methods for some of the recipes can be a little time-consuming, even though they're essentially very easy. So it's absolutely fine to reach for shop-bought products from time to time. In fact, throughout this book you will find little tips for alternatives, to speed up even the longer recipes!

Advance preparation

Certain components lend themselves well to being made in advance. For example, you can make the shortcrust pastry for a quiche or tart the day before and leave it in the fridge overnight. Yeast dough is also great to make in advance. Once you've kneaded it, you can keep it in the fridge for up to 24 hours. Even entire recipes like lasagne can be made the day before, so that all you have to do on the day is pop it in the oven. Certain fillings or mixtures actually work better when made in advance, such as the one for the courgette and chickpea burger (p. 155). Chilling them takes some of the moisture out, making them easier to work with and shape. If you don't have time to wait though, you can always add a little flour instead.

Ingredient swaps

I rarely use highly processed ingredients like vegan meat substitutes. Instead I prefer to use mushrooms, as they have a meaty texture and delicious flavour. However, you can pretty much use any vegetables you like for my recipes, or even add pulses like lentils and chickpeas as a source of protein. It would be such a shame not to try a recipe simply because you don't like one of the ingredients or don't have any at home. I change my basic recipes here and there too. In fact, this is often how I stumble across great new recipe ideas!

My tip for great pasta

My secret tip for creamy sauces is to save the water that you've cooked your pasta or potatoes in and mix it into your sauce. The starch from the pasta binds the liquid really quickly, making the sauce wonderfully thick and creamy! And if you want to give the pasta itself a lift, simply stir in a little olive oil after draining. This stops the pasta from sticking together and gives it a fruity Italian flavour!

Vegan cheese alternatives

If the majority of your diet is made up of unprocessed plant-based foods, it won't do you any harm to have a little shop-bought vegan cheese every once in a while. Nonetheless, my homemade vegan cheese sauce recipe takes no time at all and makes a great cheese substitute for all sorts of dishes. Whether you serve it with pasta or vegetables, or use it for grilling, this 'cheese' sauce is really versatile. For grilling, the yeast melt (from the potato and broccoli bake recipe, p. 108) and the béchamel sauce (from the lentil and courgette lasagne recipe, p. 105) also make even quicker alternatives.

A well-stocked fridge

I have to say, I'm a big fan of making individual components for my recipes in advance. In particular, sauces, fresh pesto, dips and vegan cheese alternatives keep really well in sealed jars in the fridge for a few days. I usually keep my fridge well-stocked with vegan sour cream, vegan parmesan, my favourite vegan cheese sauce and either some tasty tofu feta or deliciously smooth and creamy mini mozzarella balls. Some of these recipes are quite similar to the 'Basics' chapter in my first book but – because they're so essential and difficult to substitute – I'm going to start by showing you my five favourite basic recipes as an added bonus on top of the other 70 recipes!

Basics

Cashew nut sour cream

5 mins + soaking time
Makes approx. 340 g (12 oz)

150 g (5 oz) cashew nuts
  (raw and unsalted)
150 ml (⅔ cup) water
2 tbsp. lemon juice
1 tsp. apple cider vinegar
  or white wine vinegar (optional)
½ tsp. yellow mustard
1 tbsp. nutritional yeast flakes
  (optional)
½ tsp. salt

1. Soak the cashew nuts overnight in cold water or – for the quicker version – for 20–30 minutes in hot water. Alternatively, you can boil them for 15 minutes.

2. Once the cashew nuts are soft enough to purée, pour away the soaking liquid, rinse the nuts with fresh water and leave to drain.

3. Place all the ingredients in a high-powered blender and blend until smooth.

Top tip
If you transfer the cashew nut sour cream into a clean, sealed container, it will keep for up to a week in the fridge. It becomes thicker and thicker over time. To thin it out, simply stir in a little unsweetened plant milk or water until it reaches the desired consistency

Vegan cheese sauce

15 mins
Makes 1 jar

1 medium potato
1 carrot
80 g (3 oz) cashew nuts
300 ml (1⅓ cups) water
  (or more if needed)
1 tsp. olive oil (or canola oil)
1 onion (or 2 tsp. onion powder)
3 garlic cloves (or 1 tsp. garlic
  powder)
4 tbsp. nutritional yeast flakes
  (for the cheesy flavour)
2 tsp. yellow mustard
  (or white miso paste)
1 tsp. ground paprika (optional)
approx. 1 tsp. salt, to taste
2 tsp. lemon juice
  (or white wine vinegar)
1 tbsp. tapioca starch (optional)

1. Peel and finely chop the potato and carrot. Then add to a saucepan along with the cashew nuts and 300 ml (1⅓ cups) of water. Boil for about 10 minutes or until soft enough to purée.

2. While that's boiling, heat the oil in a frying pan over a medium heat. Peel and chop the onion and fry for approx. 3 minutes with a pinch of salt. Peel and chop the garlic and add it to the pan. Fry for another minute. (If you're using powdered onion and garlic, you can skip this step.)

3. Once the potatoes are cooked, carefully transfer the contents of the pan to a blender along with the onion, garlic, yeast flakes, mustard, ground paprika, the rest of the salt and the lemon juice, and blend until creamy. If the mixture is too thick, add more water until it reaches the desired consistency. Give the sauce a little taste and add more seasoning if required.

4. The cheese sauce can be served straight away with pasta or vegetables, or simply as a dip. If you like your sauce a little cheesier or want to use it for grilling, try mixing in 1 tbsp. tapioca starch. Return the mixture to the pan and simmer for 1–2 minutes, stirring continuously, until the mixture has thickened up and is nice and 'cheesy'.

Tips and variations
- I prefer to use cashew nuts for this recipe as they have a relatively neutral flavour. However, feel free to use other nuts such as blanched almonds or macadamia nuts instead.
- You can also make a nut-free version using sunflower seeds or tahini (sesame paste), although this will affect the taste. Another good nut-free option is to use vegan cream cheese made from soya (rather than cashews) and unsweetened soya milk (instead of water).
- The sauce is great for making in advance as it keeps well in the fridge for up to a week. You can freeze it too.

Tofu feta

5 mins + soaking time
Makes 200 g (7 oz)

200 g (7 oz) firm tofu
120 ml (½ cup) olive oil
1 tbsp. dried basil
1 tbsp. dried oregano
1 tsp. dried thyme
2 garlic cloves, chopped
1 ½ tsp. sea salt
1 tsp. chilli flakes (optional)
1 tsp. whole peppercorns
 (optional)

1. Drain the tofu, pat dry and cut into cubes. Transfer the cubes of tofu into a jar with a lid.

2. Combine the rest of the ingredients for the marinade. Pour the marinade over the tofu cubes and seal the jar tightly. Shake well, so that the tofu is well-coated with the marinade. Leave the tofu feta to marinate at least overnight in the fridge (the longer you leave it, the tastier it will be).

Top tip
Feel free to vary the ingredients for the marinade according to your personal taste. For a more savoury flavour, try adding 1 tsp. white miso paste or 2–3 tbsp. nutritional yeast flakes or soy sauce. For a more acidic flavour, try adding a little vinegar or lemon juice.

Vegan mini mozzarella balls

35 mins + soaking time
Makes 50 balls

150 g (5 oz) cashew nuts
250 g (1 cup) soya yoghurt
  (unsweetened)
1½ tsp. salt
2 tbsp. nutritional yeast
  flakes (optional)
squeeze of lemon juice
  (optional)
3 tbsp. tapioca starch
1 tbsp. pure agar powder
120 ml (½ cup) water

1. Boil the cashew nuts in water for 10 minutes until softened (or soak overnight). Drain and rinse with fresh water.

2. Shake off any excess water and place the cashew nuts in a blender along with the soya yoghurt and salt (plus the yeast flakes and lemon juice, to taste) and blend until creamy. Add the tapioca starch and mix until everything is well combined. Transfer the creamy cashew mixture into a bowl and scrape out the blender using a silicone spatula.

3. In a small saucepan, mix the agar with 120 ml (½ cup) cold water until dissolved. Slowly bring to the boil and then simmer for 2–3 minutes, stirring continuously (or follow the instructions on the packet).

4. Stir the creamy cashew mixture into the pan and simmer for around 5 minutes, stirring continuously, until the mixture is very thick.

5. Fill a large bowl with ice-cold water. Using a melon baller, scoop little balls of the mozzarella mixture out of the pan and carefully place in the water. (The mixture is very sticky, so it's best to use a teaspoon or another melon baller, rather than your hands, to help you transfer the mixture.)

Continued on the next page ▶

Tips and variations

- The tapioca starch gives the mozzarella a slightly rubbery consistency like real cheese, so it's best not to substitute it with another type of starch.
- This vegan mozzarella is ideal for grilling because it melts when heated.

6. Leave to stand briefly until the mozzarella is firm. Then transfer to a lidded container and cover with salted water. The balls will keep in the fridge for up to a week.

Vegan parmesan

5 mins
Makes 200 g (1 cup)

150 g (5 oz) cashew nuts
4 tbsp. nutritional
  yeast flakes
1 tsp. sea salt
½ tsp. garlic powder

1. Place all the ingredients into a food processor and blitz until the mixture has a consistency similar to that of grated parmesan. Transfer to a clean jar, seal tightly and store in the fridge for up to 3 or 4 weeks.

Easy tips for great dough

You can rustle up so many delicious dishes using shortcrust pastry and yeast dough. Sadly, lots of people think it's hard work making your own dough, and yet all you need are a few basic ingredients and a little kneading time. In fact, once you get around to trying it, you will see for yourself just how easy it is. To make things even simpler, here are a few tips and tricks for how to make your dough properly and what to look out for so that nothing goes wrong.

Shortcrust pastry

Shortcrust is a really low-maintenance dough that's great to make in advance and keeps well in the fridge. It's also quick and easy to make, as all you have to do is combine a few ingredients. The key is to use cold ingredients and leave the dough to rest in the fridge for around 30 minutes after you've made it. This makes it firmer and easier to work with. Otherwise, the dough will be very sticky and you'll find it hard to roll it out. If you wrap it tightly in cling film, the dough will keep in the fridge for as long as 5 days, or in the freezer for up to 3 months. To defrost it, simply leave it in the fridge overnight.

Why do you have to blind-bake shortcrust pastry?
Shortcrust tastes best when it's nice and crispy, so some recipes call for it to be 'blind-baked', i.e. baked in advance with no filling. Because the fat in the dough melts in the heat of the oven, the dough can quickly sag around the sides of the baking tin. To prevent this, you weigh down the dough with dried goods such as rice, beans or chickpeas (something which is actually much less complicated than it may seem). You will find a step-by-step guide including photos in the panna cotta tart recipe (p. 215).

Continued on the next page ▶

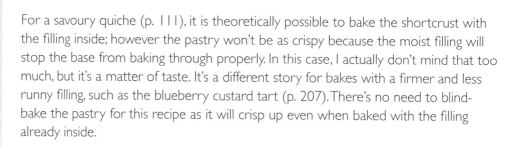

For a savoury quiche (p. 111), it is theoretically possible to bake the shortcrust with the filling inside; however the pastry won't be as crispy because the moist filling will stop the base from baking through properly. In this case, I actually don't mind that too much, but it's a matter of taste. It's a different story for bakes with a firmer and less runny filling, such as the blueberry custard tart (p. 207). There's no need to blind-bake the pastry for this recipe as it will crisp up even when baked with the filling already inside.

So why not give it a go? It's a lot easier than you might think!

Yeast dough

Yeast dough requires a little more effort than shortcrust pastry, but it's worth it for such a wonderfully light and fluffy bake. Also, it's really only the kneading that's hard work, as the rest takes care of itself.

Why do we have to knead yeast dough?
Kneading is important because it allows the gluten to form, giving the dough strength and structure. This allows the dough to retain the gases released from the yeast when it proves. Proving involves various enzymatic processes, which ultimately ensures that the dough rises.

Why does yeast dough need time to prove?
We prove yeast dough – i.e. leave it to rest – so that it rises. Most yeast doughs like to prove in a warm place, but not too warm – around 40°C (100°F) is ideal. Once the dough has doubled in size – which usually takes between 30 minutes and 1 hour – it's ready to use for your chosen recipe.

Making yeast dough in advance
You can absolutely make your yeast dough the day before. Simply follow the recipe to make your dough, then cover it with a tea towel and place it in the fridge. Yeast takes longer to expand in the fridge, so the dough won't rise as quickly. The next day, leave the dough to stand for 20 to 30 minutes at room temperature before using it for your chosen recipe.

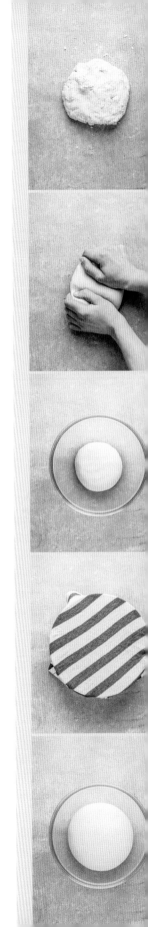

Freezing yeast dough

When I make yeast dough, I usually do lots in one go, divide it into portions and pop it in the freezer. That way, I always have some homemade dough ready to go. So if I fancy making a quick pizza or pizza pockets with samosa-style filling (p. 149) at the weekend, or I want to rustle up a vegan naan bread (p. 151) to go with my curry, I can do in no time at all.

It's that easy!

Simply make the yeast dough according to the recipe. (The naan bread is made a little differently to the basic recipe (p. 149)). Then dust with a little flour, place in a freezer bag or container and store in the freezer. It will keep for around 6 months at −18°C (0°F). When you're ready to use it, leave the dough to defrost overnight in the fridge or in a covered bowl. Then let the yeast dough prove as usual and it's ready to use for whatever recipe you fancy.

Breakfast

Granola tartlets

35 mins + time to cool
Makes 6–8

200 g (2¼ cups) rolled oats
150 g (1 cup) flaked almonds
   (or other finely chopped nuts
   or sunflower seeds/pumpkin
   seeds)
1 tsp. cinnamon (optional)
1 tbsp. cocoa powder (optional)
70 g (5 tbsp.) coconut oil
4 tbsp. maple syrup (or another
   syrup)
½ tsp. vanilla extract (optional)

For the filling (optional)
500 ml (2 cups) plant milk
5 tbsp. cornflour
1 tsp. vanilla extract
approx. 3 tbsp. sugar, to taste

1. Preheat the oven to 180°C (350°F).

2. Place the oats and flaked almonds (or other nuts/seeds) in a food processor or blender and grind coarsely. Transfer to a mixing bowl. Add the cinnamon and mix everything together. (If you're making chocolate granola, add the cocoa powder too.)

3. Melt the coconut oil in a small bowl. Add to the oat and almond mixture along with the maple syrup and vanilla extract and combine well to form a dough.

4. Divide the mixture into 6–8 lightly greased tartlet tins and press down firmly.

5. Bake the tartlets for around 15 minutes until they're just turning golden brown. Leave to cool and then carefully press them out.

6. Take 5 tbsp. of the plant milk and combine with the cornflour and vanilla extract and sweeten to taste. Pour the rest of the milk into a saucepan and bring to the boil. Whisk in the cornflour mixture and simmer until the mixture has thickened to the consistency of custard, stirring continuously. Remove from the heat and leave to cool completely. Then divide the mixture into the cooled tartlet cases and set aside for the filling to set.

7. Decorate the granola tartlets with your favourite fresh fruit and serve straight away.

Tips and variations
- Once you have filled the tartlets with the filling (or just yoghurt, if you prefer), make sure you eat them on the same day, otherwise the cases will go soggy. Unfilled, the cases for the granola tartlets will keep for up to a week at room temperature.
- You can also use this recipe to make granola-style muesli. To do this, simply take the mixture you have in step 4, and spread it out on a baking tray lined with baking paper. Bake for around 20–25 minutes, mixing halfway through, until the granola is golden brown. It will keep for up to 3 weeks, sometimes more, stored in a sealed container at room temperature.

Semolina pudding

10 mins
Makes 1 portion

500 ml (2 cups) plant milk
  (of your choice)
60 g (⅓ cup) semolina
1–2 tbsp. cashew butter
  (or alternative nut butter)
1–2 tbsp. agave syrup (or other
  syrup of your choice)
½ tsp. vanilla extract
fresh fruit (for the topping)
cinnamon (optional)

1. Pour the plant milk into a saucepan and bring to the boil. Remove from the heat and reduce the temperature.

2. Gradually add the semolina to the hot milk, return the pan to the hob and simmer for around 3 minutes over a low heat, stirring continuously.

3. Stir in the cashew butter, agave syrup and a drop of vanilla extract. Then turn off the hob, cover the pan with a lid and leave to stand for another 2–3 minutes until the semolina has swelled up.

4. Give the semolina another good stir and season to taste. Spoon into a dish and serve with fresh fruit and a pinch of cinnamon.

Vanilla porridge

15 mins
Makes 1 portion

500 ml (2 cups) plant milk
   (of your choice)
1½ tbsp. cornflour
approx. ⅓ tsp. vanilla extract,
   to taste
75 g (1 cup) fine oats
1 mashed banana or 1 grated
   apple
1 tbsp. agave syrup (or your
   preferred sweetener)
vanilla extract, to taste
cinnamon, to taste

Topping (according to your preference)
1–2 tbsp. nut butter
vegan chocolate
fruit

1. Pour the plant milk into a saucepan and bring to the boil. Remove from the heat.

2. Combine the cornflour with the vanilla extract and a little plant milk or water in a small bowl and stir into the hot milk.

3. Add the oats and bring everything back to the boil, stirring continuously.

4. Add the banana or apple and the agave syrup and season to taste with vanilla extract and cinnamon.

5. Place a lid over the pan and leave to stand for around 5 minutes.

6. Give the porridge another good stir and spoon into a dish.

7. Serve with your preferred topping, such as nut butter, chocolate pieces or fresh fruit, and enjoy!

Chocolate and banana pancakes

15 mins
Makes 6–8 pancakes

125 g (1 cup) flour (e.g. plain
   flour, spelt, oat or gluten-free
   flour)
3 tbsp. cocoa powder
1½ tsp. baking powder
1 very ripe banana, mashed
180 ml (¾ cup) plant milk (e.g.
   almond or soya milk)
2 tsp. vegetable oil (or melted
   coconut oil or nut butter)
1 tsp. maple syrup (or another
   sweetener)
oil for frying

For the topping (optional)
vegan chocolate chips or chunks
fruit of your choice

1. In a mixing bowl, combine the flour, cocoa powder and baking powder using a whisk. Place to one side.

2. Mash the banana with a fork. Transfer to a measuring jug along with the milk, oil and maple syrup and mix well. Gradually add the flour mixture and give everything a quick mix to form a batter. (If needed, add a little more sweetener or a little more liquid to thin the batter out. If you like, you can also fold in 2 tbsp. chocolate chips or blueberries).

3. Heat a little oil in a large non-stick frying pan over a medium heat.

4. Spoon 2 tbsp. of batter per pancake into the pan and fry for around 3 minutes until little bubbles start to form on the surface. Turn the pancakes over and fry for around 2–3 minutes on the other side.

5. Serve drizzled with melted chocolate and whichever fruit you prefer, or other toppings like ice cream.

Tips and variations
- For a gluten-free version, I recommend using exactly the same quantity of gluten-free flour mix.
- If you're using a heavier flour like oat or wholemeal, the pancakes won't be as light and fluffy as with plain flour. If necessary, adjust the quantity of liquid and add more milk, as different types of flour absorb different amounts of liquid.
- Canola oil works well for pancakes, but you can also use another mild-flavoured oil, melted coconut oil or vegan butter. Coconut oil sets quickly when combined with cold ingredients, so you may find it easier to use a runnier oil. Nut butters like cashew, almond or peanut butter also work well – and taste great too!

Overnight oats with berry compote

10 mins + time to cool
Makes 2 small jars

For the overnight oats
80 g (1 cup) fine oats
200 ml (1 cup) plant milk
   (of your choice)
1 tbsp. almond butter or alternative nut butter (optional)
1 tbsp. agave syrup (or other
   sweetener)
vanilla extract, to taste
cinnamon, to taste

For the berry compote
125 ml (½ cup) + 2 tbsp. cherry
   juice (or another red fruit juice)
1 tsp. lemon juice
2 tbsp. agave syrup
dash of vanilla extract
2 tsp. cornflour
150 g (1 cup) frozen mixed
   berries

Overnight oats
1. Place the oats in a container and cover with the plant milk, almond butter and agave syrup. Combine well and leave in the fridge overnight.

2. The next morning, season to taste with vanilla extract and cinnamon, and serve with the berry compote.

Berry compote
1. In a saucepan, combine 125 ml (½ cup) of cherry juice with the lemon juice, agave syrup and vanilla extract and bring to the boil.

2. In a small cup, dissolve the cornflour into the remaining 2 tbsp. of cherry juice. Stir into the pan of juice.

3. Add the frozen berries and simmer for around 2–3 minutes, until the berries are hot and the compote is nice and thick. Serve immediately with the overnight oats or leave to cool and transfer to a sealed jar. Store in the fridge until you're ready to serve.

The best ever banana bread

55 mins
Makes 1 loaf

2 ripe bananas
120 ml (½ cup) maple syrup
4 tbsp. coconut oil, melted
    (or vegan butter), plus extra
    for greasing
4 tbsp. plant milk
1 tbsp. apple cider vinegar
2 tbsp. walnuts
2 tbsp. cashew nuts
70 g (1 cup) fine oats (or more)
170 g (1⅓ cups) wholemeal flour
1½ tsp. baking powder
½ tsp. cinnamon
pinch of salt
25 g (1 oz) vegan chocolate chips

For the topping
1 banana
maple syrup
vegan chocolate chips (optional)

1. Preheat the oven to 180°C (350°F). Brush a 20 cm (8 inch) loaf tin with a little oil and set aside.

2. In a large bowl, mash the bananas and mix with the maple syrup, coconut oil, milk and apple cider vinegar.

3. Crush the walnuts and cashews and stir into the mixture along with the oats, flour, baking powder, cinnamon and salt. Finally, stir in the chocolate chips.

4. Spoon the batter into the loaf tin and smooth over the top.

5. For the topping, halve the bananas and lay them on top of the batter. Press them down slightly and drizzle with a little maple syrup.

6. Bake the loaf uncovered for 30 minutes. Then reduce the heat to 150°C (300°F) and bake for a further 20 minutes. (If the loaf starts to darken too much, cover with a piece of baking paper or foil.)

7. Leave to cool for around 30 minutes before carefully removing from the tin.

8. Once the loaf has cooled, you can sprinkle more chocolate chips over the top.

9. If wrapped, the loaf will keep in the fridge for around 3–4 days or in the freezer for 4–6 weeks.

Tips and variations
- The maple syrup can be replaced with coconut syrup, date syrup, agave syrup, raw cane sugar or standard white sugar.
- For a fluffier loaf, I would recommend using a light flour like spelt flour rather than fine oats and wholemeal flour.
- Feel free to use whatever type of nuts you prefer or even sesame seeds.

Simple buckwheat and chia loaf

1.5 hours + time to cool
Makes 1 loaf

40 g (4 tbsp.) chia seeds
240 ml (1 cup) water
300 g (2⅓ cups) buck-
  wheat flour
3 tsp. baking powder
1½ tsp. salt
160 ml (⅔ cup) water
60 ml (¼ cup) canola oil
  (or another runny oil)

Topping (optional)
35 g (2½ tbsp.) sunflower
  seeds

1. Mix the chia seeds with 240 ml (1 cup) of water in a bowl. Leave to stand for 20 minutes until it forms a gel-like consistency.

2. Combine the flour, baking powder and salt in a mixing bowl (or food processor). Add the remaining 160 ml (⅔ cup) of water, the canola oil and the chia seed mixture and give everything a quick mix to form a batter. (It's really important not to mix the batter for too long; otherwise the loaf won't rise as well and won't be as light and fluffy.) Leave to stand for around 10 minutes.

3. Preheat the oven to 180°C (350°F). Lightly grease a 20 cm (8 inch) loaf tin and line with baking paper, leaving a little extra paper hanging over each side.

4. Transfer the sticky batter to the loaf tin and smooth over the top. If you like, you can sprinkle sunflower seeds over the top. Bake for around 1 hour 10 minutes. You'll know it's baked through when a wooden skewer comes out clean.

5. Remove from the oven and leave to cool completely. Carefully lift the loaf out of the tin using the excess paper and cut into slices.

Continued on the next page ▶

Tips and variations

- The loaf will keep well for up to a week in the fridge, or even longer in the freezer.
- You can use shop-bought buckwheat flour or make it yourself. I tend to use buckwheat flakes (which look a little like fine oats) and simply blitz them for a few seconds in the blender to turn them into flour. Alternatively, you can finely grind buckwheat groats or whole buckwheat in a food processor, coffee grinder or blender.
- You can use a little less oil for this recipe if you prefer, but the loaf won't turn out quite as moist.
- Feel free to mix your favourite nuts, grains or seeds into the batter or sprinkle them over the loaf as a topping. My favourites include: chopped walnuts, hazelnuts, sunflower seeds, pumpkin seeds and poppy seeds.

Marbled waffles

20 mins
Makes 4 waffles

90 g (⅔ cup) spelt flour
1 tsp. baking powder
cinnamon (optional)
1 ripe banana, mashed
approx. 90 ml (⅓ cup) plant milk
　+ a little extra if required
1 tbsp. almond butter (or a dif-
　ferent nut butter, canola oil or
　melted coconut oil)
a little vanilla extract (optional)
1 tsp. agave syrup + a little extra
　to taste
a splash of mineral water (or
　1 tsp. apple cider vinegar)
2 tsp. cocoa powder
coconut oil to grease the
　waffle iron

1. In a mixing bowl, use a whisk to combine the flour, baking powder and cinnamon (if using).

2. Mix together the banana, plant milk, almond butter, vanilla extract and agave syrup in a mixing jug.

3. Add the banana mixture to the dry ingredients. Then add the mineral water and give everything a quick stir to form a creamy batter. (If the mixture is too thick, you can always add more plant milk.)

4. Return half the batter to the mixing jug. Add the cocoa powder to this half and combine to make a chocolate batter.

5. Preheat the waffle iron and brush with a little oil.

6. Dollop alternate spoonfuls of plain and chocolate batter into the waffle iron and bake until golden. Repeat until all the batter has been used up. Add your favourite toppings and enjoy!

Oaty raspberry muffins

45 mins + time to cool
Makes 12 muffins

250 g (3 cups) fine oats
2 tsp. baking powder
1 tsp. cinnamon
¼ tsp. salt
2 ripe bananas
250 ml (1 cup) oat milk
  (or any other plant milk)
2 tbsp. maple syrup + a little
  extra to taste
80 ml (⅓ cup) canola oil
  (or melted coconut oil)
1 tsp. vanilla extract
120 g (4 oz) raspberries
  (fresh or frozen)
icing sugar for dusting (optional)

For the crumble topping

20 g (1½ tbsp.) vegan butter
  (or coconut oil)
4 tbsp. oats
1 tbsp. coconut syrup (or another
  sugar/syrup)

1. Preheat the oven to 180°C (350°F) and line a muffin tray with paper cases.

2. For the crumble topping, place the vegan butter, oats and coconut syrup in a bowl and rub together with your hands. Place in the fridge to use later.

3. For the muffin batter, mix together the oats, baking powder, cinnamon and salt in a bowl.

4. Place the bananas on a plate and mash with a fork. Transfer the mashed banana to a bowl and mix in the oat milk, maple syrup, oil and vanilla extract.

5. Add the banana mixture to the oat mixture and combine to form a batter.

6. Divide the batter between the muffin cases. Then press 3–5 raspberries per muffin into the batter and sprinkle with the crumble mixture.

7. Bake the muffins for around 30 minutes until golden brown. Leave to cool for 10–15 minutes before removing from the tin.

8. Dust with icing sugar before serving and enjoy!

Tips and variations

- If you're using frozen raspberries, don't defrost them beforehand; otherwise they'll be watery. Simply press them into the muffin batter still frozen.
- The muffins will keep in the fridge for up to 5 days. Remember that coconut oil solidifies in the fridge. That's why I recommend using canola oil or sunflower oil so that they stay soft and fluffy.

Pasta, noodles and gnocchi

Fettuccine with red pepper sauce 51

Creamy mushroom pasta 53

Pasta with cauliflower sauce and vegetables 54

Asian-style chilli noodles 57

Spaghetti with lentil bolognese 58

Spaghetti with red pesto and mini mozzarella balls 60

Pasta with rocket and walnut pesto and cannellini beans 62

Creamy squash pasta 64

Gnocchi with pea pesto 66

Pan-fried gnocchi with savoy cabbage and mushrooms 68

Fettuccine with red pepper sauce

40 mins
Makes 2 portions

1 onion
3–4 garlic cloves
2 red peppers
1 tbsp. olive oil
250 g (9 oz) fettuccine or
   your preferred pasta
120 ml (½ cup) plant milk
   (unsweetened)
3–4 tbsp. cashew butter
   (or almond butter/sesame
   paste)
2 tbsp. tomato purée
3–4 tbsp. nutritional yeast
   flakes
approx. 1 tsp. salt, to taste
hot paprika or chilli powder,
   to taste

To garnish (optional)
fresh parsley
roasted peanut

1. Preheat the oven to 220°C (425°F).

2. Peel the onion and garlic. Chop the onion into quarters but leave the garlic cloves whole. Halve the peppers and remove the seeds. Wash the peppers and cut into strips.

3. Lay the peppers, onion and garlic cloves onto a baking tray, drizzle with a little oil and roast in the oven for around 20 minutes.

4. While they're roasting, cook the pasta in a pan of salted water until al dente, according to the packet instructions. Then drain off the water.

5. Place the roasted vegetables in a blender along with the plant milk, cashew butter, tomato purée, yeast flakes, salt and a pinch of ground paprika and blend until smooth and creamy (you can also use a stick blender).

6. Transfer the red pepper sauce to a saucepan, bring to the boil and leave to simmer for a short while until the sauce has reached the desired consistency. Taste and add more seasoning, if required. (If the sauce is too thick, you can always add a little more plant milk to thin it out.)

7. Stir the pasta into the sauce.

8. Spoon the pasta onto plates and garnish with fresh parsley and roasted peanuts.

Creamy mushroom pasta

25 mins
Makes 4 portions

300 g (10½ oz) pasta of
    your choice (you can also
    use gluten-free pasta)
2 tbsp. canola oil (or
    olive oil) + a little extra
1 onion, chopped
4 garlic cloves, chopped
500 g (1 lb) mushrooms,
    sliced
80 ml (⅓ cup) dry white
    wine (optional)
360 ml (1½ cups)
    vegetable stock
3 tbsp. soy sauce
    (or tamari)
3 tbsp. flour (or gluten-free
    flour or 2 tbsp. cornflour)
2 tsp. yellow mustard
    (optional)
2–3 tbsp. nutritional yeast
    flakes (optional)
360 ml (1½ cups) plant
    milk
1 tsp. ground paprika
    (optional)
salt and pepper

To garnish (optional)
vegan parmesan (p. 18)
fresh parsley (or thyme)

1. Using the packet instructions, cook the pasta in salted water until al dente. Drain well and stir in a little oil so that it doesn't stick together.

2. In a large frying pan, heat 1 tbsp. oil and fry the onions for 3 minutes, stirring occasionally.

3. Add the rest of the oil, along with the garlic and mushrooms, and fry for another 5–7 minutes or until the mushrooms are nicely browned. If using, deglaze the pan with the white wine, give everything a stir and then leave to reduce for a short time.

4. Mix together the vegetable stock, soy sauce and flour in a measuring jug. Then add to the pan, along with the mustard and yeast flakes. Stir in the plant milk and bring to the boil. Reduce the heat a little and allow the sauce to simmer for around 5–10 minutes or until it has reached the desired consistency. Season with ground paprika, salt and pepper.

5. Add the cooked pasta to the pan, stir it into the sauce and, if necessary, let everything warm through.

6. Garnish with vegan parmesan and parsley and dig in!

Top tip
Gluten-free option: Use gluten-free pasta or serve the mushroom sauce with rice, quinoa or mashed potatoes.

Pasta with cauliflower sauce and vegetables

20 mins
Makes 4 portions

500 g (1 lb) pasta of your choice
1 tbsp. olive oil + a little extra
600 g (1 lb 5 oz) cauliflower
300 ml (1¼ cups) vegetable stock
1 onion, peeled and finely
   chopped
4 garlic cloves, peeled and
   chopped
approx. 250 ml (1 cup) plant milk
   (unsweetened)
2 tsp. salt
3–4 tbsp. nutritional yeast flakes
pepper

To serve (optional)
1–2 tbsp. olive oil
½ courgette, thinly sliced
250 g (9 oz) mushrooms
200 g (7 oz) cherry tomatoes
fresh basil
fresh parsley

1. Follow the instructions on the packet to cook the pasta al dente. Then drain off the water. Stir a little olive oil into the pasta so that it doesn't stick together.

2. Break the cauliflower into small florets and cook in the vegetable stock for around 10–12 minutes.

3. While that's cooking, heat the olive oil in a frying pan and fry the onions for around 3 minutes until translucent. Add the garlic and fry for another minute. Remove from the pan and add to the cauliflower. Add the plant milk, salt, yeast flakes and pepper and purée to form a creamy sauce. If required, add more plant milk to get the right consistency.

4. Using the same frying pan, heat the rest of the oil. Fry the courgette and mushrooms for around 3 minutes over a high heat. Add the tomatoes and sweat over a low heat for another 2–3 minutes.

5. Stir the pasta into the sauce and season to taste with salt, pepper and any other seasoning you fancy.

6. Serve with the fried vegetables and fresh herbs.

Asian-style chilli noodles

20 mins
Makes 2 portions

200 g (7 oz) whole wheat
    or rice ribbon noodles
2 tbsp. sweet and sour
    sauce
2 spring onions
a small piece of ginger
2 garlic cloves
1 red pepper
150 g (5 oz) mushrooms
1–2 tbsp. sesame oil
2 tbsp. soy sauce or tamari
120 ml (½ cup) coconut
    milk
1 tsp. agave syrup
    (optional)
chilli flakes, to taste
salt and pepper

To garnish (optional)
1 lime
2 tbsp. toasted sesame
    seeds
2 tbsp. black sesame seeds

1. Cook the noodles according to the packet instructions. Drain and stir in the sweet and sour sauce.

2. While the noodles are cooking, chop and stir-fry the vegetables. Slice the spring onions into thin rings, keeping the green and white parts separate. Peel and finely chop the ginger and garlic. Halve the pepper and remove the seeds. Then wash it and cut it into strips. Clean and slice the mushrooms.

3. Heat the oil in a frying pan. Sweat the white parts of the spring onions along with the ginger and garlic for around 1–2 minutes. Add the pepper and mushrooms and fry for around 5 minutes. Fold in the noodles and stir-fry everything for a little longer. (If you like your noodles a little crispier, you can fry them for longer.) Douse with the soy sauce and coconut milk. Season with agave syrup, chilli flakes, salt and pepper and leave to simmer for a short while.

4. Stir the noodles through the sauce and season again.

5. Cut the lime into wedges. Dish the noodles into bowls and arrange the lime wedges on the side. Sprinkle with the green spring onions and sesame seeds.

Spaghetti with lentil bolognese

25 mins
Makes 2 portions

1 tbsp. olive oil
1 onion, chopped
1 carrot, chopped
1 small stick of celery (optional)
100 g (3½ oz) mushrooms,
   chopped
1 tbsp. tomato purée
salt and pepper
2 tsp. Italian herbs
1 tsp. raw cane sugar (optional)
2 garlic cloves, chopped
125 g (⅔ cup) red lentils
250 g (1¼ cups) passata
200 g (1 cup) chopped tomatoes
240 ml (1 cup) vegetable stock
125 g (4½ oz) spaghetti
   (gluten-free, if required)
vegan parmesan (p. 18) or
   nutritional yeast flakes
fresh herbs (of your choice)

1. Heat the oil in a large frying pan over a medium heat. Add the onions and sweat for around 2 minutes until translucent.

2. Add the carrot, mushrooms and celery (if using). Fry for around 5–7 minutes.

3. Add the tomato purée, herbs, seasoning, sugar and garlic, and fry for around 1–2 minutes.

4. Add the lentils, tomatoes and vegetable stock and stir well. Bring to the boil, cover, reduce the heat and simmer for around 15–20 minutes until the lentils are cooked and the sauce is nice and thick. If necessary, add a little more water and more seasoning.

5. While the sauce is cooking, cook the spaghetti in salted water until al dente. Drain off any excess water.

6. Serve the lentil bolognese with the spaghetti. Garnish with your choice of vegan parmesan or yeast flakes and fresh herbs.

Spaghetti with red pesto and mini mozzarella balls

25 mins + soaking time
Makes 3–4 portions

400 g (14 oz) spaghetti
 (or any other type of pasta)
200 g (7 oz) cherry tomatoes,
 halved
200 g (7 oz) vegan mini
 mozzarella balls (p. 17)
toasted pine nuts to garnish
vegan parmesan (p. 18)
fresh basil (or other herbs)

For the red pesto
100 g (½ cup) sun-dried
 tomatoes
25 g (¼ cup) pine nuts
25 g (¼ cup) walnuts
 (or more pine nuts)
approx. 70 ml (5 tbsp.) olive oil
1 tbsp. tomato purée
2 garlic cloves, peeled
1 tsp. balsamic vinegar
2 tsp. Herbes de Provence
salt and pepper

1. Soak the sun-dried tomatoes in water for around 20 minutes. Then drain and roughly chop.

2. Toast the pine nuts in a dry pan for a short time. Then transfer them to a blender and purée along with all the other ingredients for the pesto (you can also use a stick blender). Season with salt and pepper.

3. Spoon the pesto into a lidded jar and cover well with olive oil. It will keep in the fridge for up to 2 weeks.

4. Cook the spaghetti according to the packet instructions. Then drain, keeping aside about half a cup of the cooking water.

5. Shake off any excess water and return the pasta to the pan. Add the pesto and stir into the pasta. If you like, you can add some of the cooking water you saved to get the right consistency.

6. Plate up and garnish with cherry tomato halves, vegan mini mozzarella balls, toasted pine nuts, vegan parmesan and basil.

Top tip
The pesto also makes a really tasty spread for bread!

Pasta with rocket and walnut pesto and cannellini beans

25 mins
Serves 2

200 g (7 oz) spaghetti
150 g (¾ cup) cannellini beans,
  rinsed and drained
pomegranate seeds
handful of rocket to garnish

For the rocket and walnut pesto
50 g (½ cup) walnuts
1 tbsp. olive oil
1 garlic clove
2 tbsp. nutritional yeast flakes
⅔ tsp. salt
100 g (3½ oz) rocket
1 tbsp. lemon juice
50 ml (¼ cup) water

1. Using the packet instructions, cook the spaghetti in plenty of salted water until al dente.

2. While the pasta is cooking, make the pesto. Toast the walnuts in a dry frying pan until lightly browned. Transfer to a chopping board and roughly chop.

3. In the same pan, heat 1 tbsp. oil. Peel and chop the garlic and fry it in the hot oil for a few seconds. Then transfer it to a blender and purée along with the rest of the ingredients for the pesto to form a paste (you can also use a stick blender). Taste and add more seasoning, if required.

4. Drain the spaghetti and stir in the cannellini beans and pesto. Garnish with pomegranate seeds and a handful of rocket.

Creamy squash pasta

15 mins
Makes 4 portions

1 small Hokkaido squash or
   butternut squash (around 800 g
   (1 lb 12 oz) or a tin of pumpkin
   purée)
400 g (14 oz) pasta (whichever
   type you prefer)
a glug of olive oil (optional)
2 garlic cloves, chopped
1 tbsp. coconut oil (or vegan
   butter)
¼ tsp. ground paprika
approx. ½ tsp. salt, to taste
5 tbsp. nutritional yeast flakes
   (for a cheesy flavour)
1 tbsp. tapioca starch (optional)
240 ml (1 cup) plant milk
3–4 tbsp. nut butter (optional)

To serve (optional)
vegan parmesan (p. 18)
fresh basil, to taste

1. Chop the squash into cubes and either bake in the oven, boil in a pan or cook in the microwave until soft. (The skin of a Hokkaido squash goes lovely and soft when cooked. If using butternut squash, you will need to peel it first because the skin is too hard).

2. Using the packet instructions, cook the pasta until al dente. Drain the pasta well and stir in a little olive oil (optional).

3. While the pasta is cooking, you can make the sauce. Start by frying the garlic in 1 tbsp. coconut oil over a moderate heat for 1 minute.

4. Add 400 g (14 oz) of the cooked squash (or pumpkin purée) to a food processor along with the garlic, paprika, salt, yeast flakes, tapioca starch, plant milk and nut butter and blend to form a creamy sauce.

5. Pour the squash sauce into a large saucepan, simmer over a moderate heat, stirring frequently, and season. (If the sauce is too thick, add a little more milk. If it's too thin, let it simmer for a bit longer.)

6. Add the cooked pasta to the sauce and give everything a good stir. Serve the pasta with vegan parmesan and fresh basil or any other toppings you like.

Tips and variations
- I strongly recommend using the tapioca starch if you want the squash sauce to be a bit thicker and 'cheesier'. You can also use cornflour to thicken it up.
- The nut butter gives the sauce a creamier consistency. I recommend cashew butter or almond butter. For a nut-free version, soya-based vegan cream cheese works well, as do pine nuts. Soak the nuts for at least 8 hours or overnight before using, or boil for 20 minutes to soften. 60 g (2 oz) cashew nuts makes about 4 tbsp. cashew butter.

Gnocchi with pea pesto

25 mins
Makes 4 portions

800 g (1 lb 12 oz) gnocchi

For the pea pesto
30 g (¼ cup) pine nuts
350 g (12 oz) frozen peas
2 garlic cloves, peeled
1 tbsp. lemon juice
1 avocado (optional)
3–4 tbsp. olive oil (or more if
   required)
handful of basil + a little extra to
   garnish
salt and pepper

1. Cook the gnocchi according to the packet instructions. Then drain off the water.

2. Toast the pine nuts in a dry pan and leave to cool.

3. Defrost the peas. Blend 200 g (7 oz) of the peas with the garlic, lemon juice, avocado, toasted pine nuts, oil and basil to form a creamy paste.

4. Season to taste with salt and pepper, and give it another good mix.

5. Stir the pesto into the gnocchi and garnish with the rest of the peas and the basil.

Top tip
The pesto also makes a really tasty spread for bread!

Pan-fried gnocchi with savoy cabbage and mushrooms

20 mins
Makes 2 portions

300 g (10 oz) mushrooms
200 g (7 oz) savoy cabbage
  (or spinach)
1 onion
2 garlic cloves
1–2 tbsp. olive oil
salt and pepper
100 ml (½ cup) vegan white wine
  (or vegetable stock)
1 tsp. yellow mustard
200 ml (1 cup) vegan cream
  (or full-fat tinned coconut milk)
250 g (9 oz) gnocchi

To garnish (optional)
nutritional yeast flakes
fresh parsley

1. Clean and slice the mushrooms.

2. Chop the cabbage and rinse it in a sieve.

3. Peel and finely chop the onion and garlic.

4. Heat the olive oil in a large frying pan. Fry the mushrooms over a high heat for 2–3 minutes until they're well-browned on each side. Reduce the heat a little and add the onion and garlic. Sweat for another 2–3 minutes, stirring occasionally. Add the cabbage, season with salt and pepper and sweat for another 1–2 minutes.

5. Pour in the white wine, stir in the mustard and bring to the boil. Then turn down the heat.

6. Add the cream to the pan, followed by the gnocchi. Simmer over a medium heat for 3–4 minutes or until the gnocchi is soft. Season again with salt and pepper.

7. Serve the gnocchi sprinkled with yeast flakes and fresh parsley.

Rice and light meals

Couscous and potato cakes with cucumber salad 74

Aubergine schnitzel with carrot purée and Brussels sprouts 76

Creamy mushroom risotto 79

Creamy sweetcorn risotto with courgettes 81

Lentil and mushroom ragout with mashed potatoes 83

Vegetable fried rice 86

Veggie bean burritos 89

Vegan omelette with spinach guacamole and mushrooms 91

Vegan chickpea 'tuna' mayo 95

Couscous and potato cakes with cucumber salad

45 mins + time to cool
Makes 4 portions (10 cakes)

For the cucumber salad
1 large cucumber
7 tbsp. soya yoghurt
  (unsweetened)
3–4 tbsp. lemon juice
salt and pepper
1 garlic clove
handful of fresh dill

For the couscous and potato cakes
400 g (14 oz) boiled floury
  potatoes
200 g (7 oz) couscous
350 ml (1½ cups) vegetable stock
1 tsp. cumin
2 tsp. ground paprika
1 tbsp. Herbes de Provence
salt and pepper
handful of fresh parsley
oil for frying
1 avocado
lemon juice for drizzling

1. Wash and thinly slice the cucumber.

2. Mix the soya yoghurt together with the lemon juice, salt and pepper. Peel and crush the garlic and add to the yoghurt mixture. Roughly chop the dill and stir that in as well. Add the sliced cucumber, mix well and season to taste. Cover the cucumber salad and leave it to stand in the fridge for around 20 minutes.

Couscous and potato cakes

1. Boil the potatoes in their skins for approx. 25 minutes until soft. Drain off the water and leave the potatoes to cool. Then carefully peel and mash them.

2. While the potatoes are cooking, place the couscous in a bowl, pour over the boiling vegetable stock, cover and leave to stand for around 10 minutes.

3. Once the couscous has absorbed all the stock, add it to the mashed potatoes and season with the cumin, paprika, Herbes de Provence and salt and pepper. Finely chop the parsley and stir that in as well.

4. With wet hands, shape the mixture into small patties.

5. Heat plenty of oil in a frying pan and fry the patties on both sides until crisp and golden.

6. While the potato cakes are frying, halve the avocado, remove the stone and scoop out the flesh. Thinly slice the avocado and drizzle with a little lemon juice.

7. Serve the couscous and potato cakes with the fresh cucumber salad and avocado..

Aubergine schnitzel with carrot purée and Brussels sprouts

35 mins
Makes 2 portions

1 aubergine
salt
1 large potato
2–3 carrots
400 g (14 oz) Brussels
  sprouts
50 g (⅓ cup) flour
80 ml (⅓ cup) plant milk
  (unsweetened)
100 g (3½ oz)
  breadcrumbs
3 tbsp. nutritional yeast
  flakes
1 tsp. ground paprika
pepper
4 tbsp. olive oil for frying
20 g (1½ tbsp.) vegan
  butter
approx. 60 ml (¼ cup)
  plant milk
salt

To garnish (optional)
pomegranate seeds
fresh herbs

1. Wash the aubergine and cut into slices approx. 7 mm (¼ inch) thick. Sprinkle with salt and leave to stand for about 10 minutes. Then pat try.

2. While you're waiting, wash, peel and dice the carrots and potato. Add to a pan of boiling salted water and cook for around 15 minutes.

3. Remove the outer leaves of the Brussels sprouts and trim off the stem. Chop the sprouts in half and boil them in the water along with the carrots and potatoes for around 3–4 minutes. Remove from the water with a slotted spoon, drain well and place to one side.

4. In a deep-sided plate, mix the flour with 80 ml (⅓ cup) of plant milk. On another plate, combine the breadcrumbs, yeast flakes, paprika and a pinch of pepper. One at a time, dip the aubergine slices into the flour and milk mixture and then coat them evenly in the breadcrumb mixture.

5. Heat 2 tbsp. oil in a large frying pan over a medium heat. Fry the breaded aubergine slices for approx. 3 minutes on each side until golden brown. Remove from the pan and place them onto a piece of kitchen paper to soak up any excess oil.

6. In the same pan, heat the remaining 2 tbsp. oil and fry the blanched Brussels sprouts for around 3 minutes until golden brown on all sides. Season to taste with salt and pepper.

7. Once the potatoes and carrots are cooked, drain off the water. Then add the vegan butter and the rest of the plant milk and either mash or purée. Season with salt and pepper.

8. Dish everything onto a plate and garnish with pomegranate seeds and fresh herbs.

Creamy mushroom risotto

25 mins
Makes 2 portions

1 onion
3 garlic cloves
1–2 tbsp. vegan butter (or olive oil)
125 g (4½ oz) risotto rice
50 ml (¼ cup) white wine (vegan)
200 ml (1 cup) vegetable stock
100 ml (½ cup) soy sauce (or coconut milk)
250 g (9 oz) mushrooms
oil for frying
soy sauce
salt and pepper
nutritional yeast flakes or vegan parmesan (p. 18), to taste

1. Finely chop the onion and garlic.

2. Heat the butter in a saucepan and fry the onions and garlic briefly.

3. Add the risotto rice and continue to fry for around 1–2 minutes.

4. Deglaze with the white wine, add the vegetable stock and simmer for around 15 minutes, stirring occasionally, until the rice has absorbed the liquid. While the rice is cooking, gradually pour in the soya cream, a little at a time.

5. Clean and slice the mushrooms.

6. Add a little oil to a frying pan and fry the mushrooms over a high heat until golden brown. Season with soy sauce and add to the risotto.

7. Finally, season the risotto to taste with salt and pepper, and serve sprinkled with yeast flakes or vegan parmesan.

Creamy sweetcorn risotto with courgettes

30 mins
Makes 3 portions

2 cobs of corn (see tip below)
840–960 ml (3½–4 cups)
    vegetable stock
2 tbsp. olive oil (for frying)
1 onion, finely diced
salt
185 g (6½ oz) Arborio rice
    (uncooked)
2 garlic cloves, chopped
60 ml (¼ cup) vegan white wine
    (or extra vegetable stock)
1 courgette, finely diced
60 g (2 oz) vegan parmesan
    (p. 18) (or a little more)
approx. ¼ tsp. black pepper, to
    taste

To serve (optional)
spring onions, chopped
fresh parsley, chopped
fresh basil, chopped

1. If you're using fresh corn on the cob, you need to blanch them in the vegetable stock for 5 minutes before using (if necessary, cut the cobs in half). Once they're cooked, turn off the hob, remove the corn from the stock and set aside to cool. Then place a lid on the pan to keep the stock warm. (If you're using cooked, tinned or frozen sweetcorn, just heat up the vegetable stock and keep it warm).

2. Heat 1 tbsp. oil in a non-stick saucepan or frying pan over a medium heat, add the onion and a pinch of salt and fry for around 5 minutes. Add the rice and fry for another 2 minutes, stirring continuously. Add the garlic and fry for another 30 seconds, still stirring. Deglaze with the white wine. Continue stirring until the wine is almost completely reduced.

3. Next add a cup of the warm vegetable stock to the rice and simmer over a low heat, stirring frequently. Once almost all of the liquid has been absorbed by the rice, add another cup of stock and continue to simmer, stirring occasionally, until that has almost completely reduced as well. Keep repeating this process until the rice is cooked through (al dente) and the risotto is nice and creamy. The whole thing should take around 25 minutes.

Continued on the next page ▶

4. While the risotto is cooking, you can fry the vegetables in a separate pan. For this, heat the rest of the oil over a medium heat. Then add the diced courgette and a pinch of salt. Fry for approx. 2 minutes until the courgette has softened and begun to brown. Cut the corn from the cobs and add to the pan with the courgette. Fry everything together for around 5 minutes, stirring occasionally, until the vegetables are nicely browned. (If you like, you can also add extra garlic and onions, or any other seasoning).

5. Once the risotto is creamy and the rice is al dente, stir in the vegan parmesan along with the courgette and sweetcorn. Season to taste with salt and pepper, and garnish with spring onions, parsley and basil. Serve warm and enjoy!

Tips and variations
- If all the stock has been used up before the risotto is ready, you can simply warm up a little water or plant milk and add that.
- Pat the sweetcorn dry before you fry it.
- To shorten the preparation time, try using cooked sweetcorn or 350 g (12 oz) tinned or frozen sweetcorn.

Lentil and mushroom ragout with mashed potatoes

40 mins
Makes 2 portions

For the lentil and mushroom ragout

1 tbsp. olive oil
1 large onion
150 g (5 oz) mushrooms
1 carrot
2 garlic cloves
150 g (5 oz) dried green or
   brown lentils
2–3 tbsp. soy sauce or tamari
2 tbsp. chopped fresh thyme
1 tbsp. tomato purée (optional)
100 ml (½ cup) red wine
470 ml (2 cups) vegetable stock
1 bay leaf (optional)
salt and pepper

To thicken (optional)

approx. 50 ml (¼ cup)
   unsweetened plant milk (or
   water)
2 tsp. cornflour

To finish (optional)

vegan cream (or full-fat coconut
   milk)

1. Heat the oil in a large, deep frying pan. Peel and chop the onion and fry for approx. 2 minutes, stirring occasionally.

2. Slice the mushrooms, add to the onion and fry for around 3–5 minutes.

3. While they're frying, peel and finely dice the carrot. Peel and finely chop the garlic. Place the lentils into a sieve and rinse under running water. Add the garlic, soy sauce, thyme, tomato purée, carrots and lentils to the mushrooms and sweat for a short time. Deglaze with the red wine and let it reduce for 1–2 minutes. Then add the vegetable stock and the bay leaf and leave to simmer over a low heat for around 20 minutes until the lentils have softened. (If necessary, add a little more stock).

4. While the lentils are cooking, peel the potatoes and cut into quarters. Boil in a large saucepan of salted water for about 12–15 minutes until they have softened.

5. Drain the potatoes, shaking off any excess water, and return them to the pan. Add the vegan butter, plant milk and salt and pepper to taste, and mash using a potato masher.

Continued on the next page ▶

For the mashed potato
3 medium potatoes
2 tbsp. vegan butter (or olive oil)
plant milk (as required)
salt and pepper

To garnish (optional)
fresh parsley
vegan parmesan (p. 18)

6. Once the lentils have softened, remove the bay leaf. Taste the sauce and season with a little more salt and pepper, if needed. (If you like your sauce a bit thicker, combine a little water or plant milk with 2 tsp. cornflour. Stir the mixture into the sauce and bring back to the boil.) For a creamier sauce, stir in a little vegan cream or coconut milk.

7. Serve the lentil and mushroom ragout on a bed of mashed potato. Garnish with fresh parsley or other herbs and a sprinkling of vegan parmesan.

Tips and variations
- The lentil and mushroom ragout will keep for up to 4 days in the fridge or up to a month in the freezer. I recommend always making fresh mashed potato because it tastes so much better!
- If you don't like mashed potato, you can serve the ragout with any kind of pasta, gnocchi, rice or even naan bread (p. 151).
- I like to use green lentils for this recipe, which takes around 20 minutes to cook. Of course, you can use any variety of lentils, such as brown, black, red or yellow. However, make sure you adjust the cooking time according to the instructions on the packet.
- You can replace the mushrooms with other vegetables such as finely diced courgette, carrots, swede, sweet potatoes, squash or peas.
- To make the ragout creamier and even more tasty, I like to add some full-fat coconut milk from a tin. Alternatively, you can also finish it off with a little vegan cream, cashew nut sour cream (p. 10) or cashew butter.
- The red wine gives the ragout a more intense flavour. However, you can leave it out and just add more vegetable stock instead.

Vegetable fried rice

15 mins + cooking time
Makes 2 portions

125 g (4½ oz) rice
100 g (3½ oz) leek (or 1 onion)
1 carrot
1 courgette
2 garlic cloves
1 tbsp. oil (peanut, sesame or
   canola oil)
250 g (9 oz) smoked tofu
60 g (2 oz) soya beans (or frozen
   peas, defrosted)
60 g (2 oz) sweetcorn, rinsed and
   drained
2–3 tbsp. tamari or soy sauce
1 tbsp. peanut butter (or sesame
   paste)
pinch of salt
chilli, to taste

To garnish
cashew nuts
fresh parsley
sesame seeds

1. Cook the rice according to the packet instructions.

2. Thinly slice the leek, carrot and courgette. Chop the garlic.

3. Heat the oil in a large frying pan and fry the tofu for around 5 minutes until golden brown. Then remove from the pan and set aside.

4. With the pan still hot, add the garlic and thinly sliced vegetables. Fry for 3–4 minutes, stirring occasionally. If needed, add a little more oil.

5. Add the rice, tofu, soya beans, sweetcorn and tamari. Fry everything over a medium heat for 3–4 minutes, stirring frequently. Finish off with a little peanut butter and season with salt and chilli.

6. Toast the cashew nuts in a dry pan. Serve the vegetable fried rice with fresh parsley, sesame seeds and toasted cashew nuts.

Top tip
You can replace the tofu with chickpeas if you prefer.

Veggie bean burritos

30 mins
Makes 6 burritos

For the sauce
200 g (1 cup) cashew nut sour
    cream (p. 10)
approx. 40 g (2½ tbsp.) tomato
    ketchup, to taste
1 garlic clove, peeled and crushed
salt and pepper
chilli, to taste
1 tsp. white wine vinegar
    (or apple cider vinegar)

For the burritos
250 g (9 oz) rice
1 onion
1 tbsp. olive oil
1 tin of kidney beans, rinsed and
    drained
1 tin of sweetcorn, rinsed and
    drained
½ tsp. cumin
salt and pepper
pinch of chilli powder (optional)
1 lettuce heart
bunch of parsley (or coriander)
2 carrots
4 radishes
1 red pepper
6 large tortilla wraps

1. Mix together all the ingredients for the sauce and store in the fridge until you're ready to serve up.

2. Cook the rice in salted water according to the packet instructions.

3. Peel and finely chop the onion. Heat the oil in a frying pan and fry the onion for approx. 3 minutes. Stir in the beans, sweetcorn, spices, salt and pepper. Season and set aside.

4. Wash the lettuce and parsley, shake off any excess water and finely chop. Peel the carrots, wash the radishes and grate them both. Halve the pepper, remove the seeds, wash and finely dice.

5. Warm the tortillas according to the packet instructions. Brush with a little sauce. Then spoon on the rice, radishes, carrots, lettuce, pepper and bean and sweetcorn mixture. Fold the sides of the tortillas over the filling and fold up the ends. Wrap the burritos in greaseproof paper and either serve straight away or keep in the fridge until later.

6. Before serving, cut the burritos in half with a sharp knife. Serve with the rest of the sauce and enjoy!

Vegan omelette with spinach guacamole and mushrooms

30 mins
Makes 1 omelette

150 g (5 oz) silken tofu
   (drained)
45 g (⅓ cup) chickpea flour
1 tsp. baking powder
2 tbsp. nutritional yeast flakes
½ tsp. salt
¼ tsp. kala namak (optional –
   gives the dish its eggy
   flavour)
¼ tsp. onion or garlic powder
½ tsp. turmeric (for the
   yellow colour)
½ tsp. sweet paprika
100 ml (½ cup) unsweetened
   soya milk (or another plant
   milk)
1–2 tsp. olive oil (for frying)

For the spinach guacamole
1 avocado
1 garlic clove
handful of fresh spinach
squeeze of lemon juice
salt and pepper (to taste)

1. Drain the tofu well and carefully pat it dry with kitchen paper. Then place in a blender along with the chickpea flour, baking powder, yeast flakes, salt, kala namak, onion powder, turmeric, paprika and soya milk, and blend well to form a smooth purée (you can also use a stick blender). Set aside for 3–5 minutes to give the mixture time to expand a little.

2. Evenly grease the base of a non-stick frying pan with 1 tsp. olive oil and heat. Pour in the omelette mixture and give the pan a little shake so that the mixture covers the base of the pan evenly. Place a lid on the pan and fry the omelette over a medium heat for around 5 minutes until the surface is no longer moist. Using a turner or spatula, carefully turn the omelette over and fry on the other side for 2–3 minutes.

Continued on the next page ▶

For the mushrooms

1 tbsp. olive oil (for frying)
150 g (5 oz) mushrooms
1 tbsp. soy sauce
  (or tamari)

Mushrooms

While the omelette is cooking, heat 1 tbsp. olive oil in a separate pan. Slice the mushrooms and fry over a high heat for around 3 minutes. Then reduce the heat a little and fry for another 2–3 minutes until the mushrooms look nice and brown. Douse with soy sauce and give the pan a shake so that the mushrooms are evenly coated. Then remove from the pan.

Spinach guacamole

1. Next, it's time to prepare the guacamole filling. To do this, halve the avocado, remove the stone, scoop out the flesh with a spoon and place in a mixing jug. Peel and crush the garlic and add it to the jug. Add the spinach, a squeeze of lemon juice and a little salt and pepper. Using a stick blender, purée until creamy and season again.

2. Spread the guacamole onto the omelette and fold in half. Arrange the fried mushrooms on top and enjoy!

Tips and variations

- This recipe also works without tofu, but it will have a slightly firmer texture. Simply leave the tofu out and, if necessary, use a little less salt or kala namak.
- Kala namak is also known as black salt, Indian black salt or Himalayan black salt. It's what gives the omelette its 'eggy' flavour, but you can just use normal salt instead. However, be aware that kala namak isn't as salty as regular salt.

Vegan chickpea 'tuna' mayo

10 mins
Makes 400 g (14 oz)

1 tin of chickpeas, rinsed and
　drained
1 gherkin, finely chopped
½ tsp. nori flakes
1 stick of celery, finely chopped
1 red onion, finely chopped
75 g (⅓ cup) vegan mayonnaise
1 tsp. yellow mustard
1 tbsp. lemon juice
¼ tsp. salt
¼ tsp. pepper
cress or whichever fresh herbs
　you prefer

1. Coarsely mash the chickpeas with a potato masher or fork.

2. Add the rest of the ingredients, mix well and season to taste. Cover and leave to stand in the fridge for at least half an hour.

3. Use generous portions of the chickpea 'tuna' mayo as a filling or topping for sandwiches, rolls or toasties. Garnish with cress or other fresh herbs and enjoy!

Top tip
If you'd rather not use shop-bought vegan mayonnaise, you can use cashew nut sour cream (p. 10) instead. Mix in 1 tbsp. pickling liquid from the gherkins and 1 crushed garlic clove.

Hearty oven bakes

Gnocchi bake

20 mins
Makes 2–3 portions

1 tbsp. olive oil
2 small onions
2 garlic cloves
1 tbsp. tomato purée
1 tin chopped tomatoes or 400 g
  (2 cups) passata
salt and pepper
Italian herbs (of your choice)
1 tsp. sugar
400 g (14 oz) gnocchi
150 g (5 oz) cherry tomatoes,
  halved
250 g (9 oz) mini mozzarella balls
  (p. 17)
fresh basil, to garnish

1. Preheat the oven to 180°C (350°F).

2. Heat the olive oil in a large oven-proof pan. Finely chop the onions and sweat in the hot pan for around 2 minutes until translucent. Crush the garlic, add to the pan and sweat for another minute.

3. Add the tomato purée and tinned tomatoes. Season with salt, pepper, Italian herbs and sugar. Stir in the gnocchi and add the cherry tomatoes. Let everything simmer for approx. 3–5 minutes until the gnocchi is cooked (you can add a little water, if necessary).

4. Arrange the mozzarella balls on top of the gnocchi and tomato sauce. Place the pan in the preheated oven and grill for around 10 minutes, until the mozzarella has melted.

5. Garnish the gnocchi bake with fresh basil and serve straight away.

Top tip
You don't have to grill the gnocchi if you prefer not to – it tastes delicious straight from the hob too!

Pasta bake with squash and spinach

30 mins
Makes 4 portions

350 g (12 oz) fusilli (or any other type of pasta)
250 g (9 oz) fresh spinach
a little olive oil for the pasta
400 g (14 oz) Hokkaido squash or butternut squash
100 g (3½ oz) cashew nuts
250 ml (1 cup) water (or more if needed)
1 tbsp. olive oil (or canola oil)
1 onion, chopped
3 garlic cloves, chopped
4 tbsp. nutritional yeast flakes, optional
approx. 1 tsp. sea salt, to taste
2 tsp. lemon juice (optional)
100 g (3½ oz) vegan cheese, grated – for the grilled cheese topping
fresh parsley, to garnish

1. Boil the pasta in a pan of salted water until al dente (about 3 minutes less than stated on the packet). At the last minute, add the spinach leaves to the pan to wilt them. Drain off the water and stir in a little oil so that the pasta doesn't stick together.

2. Preheat the oven to 180°C (350°F).

3. Cut the squash into cubes. Then add to a saucepan along with the cashew nuts and water. Boil for about 10 minutes or until everything is soft enough to purée. (The skin of a Hokkaido squash goes lovely and soft when cooked. If using butternut squash, you will need to peel it first because the skin is too hard).

4. While the squash is cooking, heat the oil in a frying pan over a medium heat and fry the onion for approx. 3 minutes. Add the garlic and fry for another minute.

5. Once the squash is cooked, carefully transfer the contents of the pan to a blender, along with the onion, garlic, yeast flakes, salt and lemon juice, and blend until creamy. If the sauce is too thick, add more water until it reaches the desired consistency. (If you prefer, you can also use a stick blender to purée everything without removing it from the saucepan. Just watch out for the mixture splattering as it could burn you.) Give the sauce a little taste and add more seasoning if required.

Continued on the next page ▶

6. Place the pasta and spinach in an oven-proof dish. Pour the squash sauce over the top and give everything a good mix. Sprinkle with vegan cheese and grill for approx. 10–15 minutes or until the cheese has melted.

7. Remove the pasta bake from the oven and sprinkle with fresh parsley.

Tips and variations

- **Nut-free version:** You can replace the cashew nuts with sunflower seeds (or sunflower seed butter). Alternatively, vegan cream cheese (e.g. soya-based) also makes a good substitute for the nuts. For a creamier sauce, try using unsweetened plant milk, full-fat tinned coconut milk or a mixture of plant milk and soya cream instead of water.
- **Cashew nuts:** There's no need to pre-soak the cashew nuts for this recipe as they will soften when you boil them (with the squash), which will make them easier to purée. You could also use ready-made cashew butter or substitute the cashews for blanched almonds or macadamias.
- **Squash:** You can substitute the squash with 1 medium-sized potato and 1 carrot or with 1 large sweet potato plus an extra 50 ml (¼ cup) of liquid.
- **How to store:** The sauce is great for making in advance as it keeps well in the fridge for up to 5 days. You can freeze it too. It's best to store it separately from the pasta as otherwise the pasta will be too mushy.

Lentil and courgette lasagne

55 mins
Makes 4–6 portions

1 tbsp. olive oil
1 onion, finely chopped
2 carrots, peeled and finely
   chopped
2 garlic cloves, crushed
2 tbsp. tomato purée
300 ml (1¼ cups)
   vegetable stock
500 g (2½ cups) passata
150 g (5 oz) red lentils
a little olive oil for greasing
   the dish
160 g (5½ oz) cashew nuts
240 ml (1 cup) water
2 tbsp. nutritional yeast
   flakes (optional, for a
   cheesy flavour)
approx. ½ tsp. salt, to taste
approx. ½ tsp. black pepper,
   to taste
2 tsp. dried mixed herbs
   (optional)
1 large courgette, sliced
6–8 lasagne sheets (dried)

1. Heat the oil in a frying pan. Add the onion and carrots and sweat for approx. 4 minutes, stirring occasionally. Then add the garlic and fry for another minute, stirring continuously, until fragrant.

2. Next add the tomato purée, vegetable stock, tomatoes and lentils, and simmer for 15 minutes, stirring occasionally, until the sauce is nice and thick. Set aside to cool a little. (If the sauce is too thick, you can add a little extra vegetable stock or passata, but no more than 100 ml (½ cup), otherwise the lasagne will be too watery.)

3. Preheat the oven to 180°C (350°F). Brush an oven-proof dish with oil.

4. Place the cashew nuts, water, yeast flakes, salt, pepper and mixed herbs in a high-powered blender (or food processor) and blend until smooth and creamy.

5. To layer the lasagne, start by spooning a quarter of the lentil and tomato sauce onto the base of the oven dish. Then lay some courgette slices on top of the sauce, drizzle over a portion of the cashew nut sauce and arrange 3–4 lasagne sheets on top. Then add another layer of lentil sauce, followed by another layer of courgette slices and more cashew sauce. Repeat this process for the next layer. If you like, you can arrange a few slices of tomato on top, drizzled with a little olive oil so that they don't dry out.

Continued on the next page ▶

For the topping (optional)
2–3 medium-sized tomatoes,
   sliced
1 tsp. olive oil for drizzling
handful of mini mozzarella balls
   (p. 17) or grated vegan cheese
   (optional)
toasted pine nuts
vegan parmesan (p. 18)
fresh basil

6. Bake the lasagne for around 30–40 minutes (if the surface is browning too quickly in the oven, cover the dish with foil).

7. If you'd like it a little cheesier, remove the lasagne from the oven after 25 minutes and sprinkle with a few mini mozzarella balls or a little grated vegan cheese. Then bake for another 10 minutes until the vegan cheese has melted and the lasagne looks deliciously golden.

8. Once cooked, leave the lasagne to cool a little so that it firms up, making it easier to slice.

9. Serve the lasagne sprinkled with toasted pine nuts, vegan parmesan, fresh basil or any other toppings of your choice, and enjoy!

Tips and variations
- If you don't have a high-powered blender, I recommend soaking the cashews for about an hour in hot water or boiling them for 15–20 minutes. This will make them softer and easier to purée.
- Instead of using cashews, you can also make your own vegan béchamel sauce. To do this, simply melt 35 g (2½ tbsp.) vegan butter in a hot pan over a medium heat. Then add 30 g (¼ cup) flour and stir continuously for 1 minute to make a roux. Stir 360 ml (1½ cups) soya milk (or another plant milk) into the roux. Season, bring to the boil and allow to simmer for 5 minutes over a low heat. Then remove from the heat and set aside.

Potato and broccoli bake

55 mins
Makes 4 portions

1 kg (2 lbs) potatoes
500 g (1 lb) broccoli
250 ml (1 cup) soya cream
1 tsp. rosemary
1 tsp. oregano
1 tsp. thyme
2 tsp. ground paprika
1 garlic clove, crushed
salt and pepper

For the yeast melt (cheese substitute)
100 g (½ cup) vegan butter
  (or margarine)
3 tbsp. flour
250 ml (1 cup) vegetable stock
6 tbsp. nutritional yeast flakes

1. Preheat the oven to 180°C (350°F).

2. Peel and dice the potatoes.

3. Wash the broccoli, break into florets and blanch for approx. 2 minutes in a little boiling water. Then drain off the water.

4. Mix the soya cream together with the herbs, paprika, garlic, salt and pepper. Pour into the pan with the broccoli. Then add the potatoes. Mix everything together with the creamy sauce and transfer to an oven-proof dish.

Yeast melt
1. Heat the vegan butter in a saucepan. Add the flour and cook for a few seconds, stirring with a whisk. As soon as the mixture turns a pale golden brown, pour in the vegetable stock and stir in the yeast flakes. Bring to the boil and then simmer for around 2 minutes, stirring continuously. Season with salt and pepper.

2. Pour the yeast melt over the broccoli and potatoes, and bake for approx. 45 minutes until golden brown.

Tomato quiche

1 hour 20 mins + time to cool
Makes enough for one
25 cm (10 inch) tart or quiche tin

250 g (2 cups) flour (e.g. plain flour, spelt or gluten-free flour)
½ tsp. salt
120 g (½ cup) vegan butter (chilled), cut into cubes
5 tbsp. cold water
400 g (14 oz) silken tofu, drained
2 tbsp. olive oil + a little extra for drizzling
2 tbsp. cornflour (or soya flour/chickpea flour)
2 garlic cloves, crushed or ¾ tsp. garlic powder
2–3 tbsp. nutritional yeast flakes (optional)
1 tsp. salt
½ tsp. kala namak (optional – gives the filling its 'eggy' flavour)
approx. 1 tsp. pepper, to taste
300 g (10 ½ oz) cherry tomatoes, halved
2 tbsp. vegan cream or soya milk (optional, for glazing the pastry)

1. Combine the flour and salt in a large bowl. Add the vegan butter, along with the water, and knead everything together with your hands until the dough clumps together. Transfer the dough to a work surface and continue to knead until it's nice and smooth. Shape the dough into a ball and flatten slightly, then wrap in cling film and place in the fridge to chill for approx. 30 minutes.

2. Once chilled, roll the dough out on a piece of cling film (or a floured work surface) so that it's slightly larger than the tart tin. Lightly grease the tin and place the dough inside it. Create a raised edge, pressing it firmly into the sides of the tin. Prick the base a few times using a fork. (The pastry can also be blind-baked (p. 19)).

3. Preheat the oven to 180°C (350°F).

4. Blend the tofu, olive oil, cornflour, garlic, yeast flakes and seasoning until the mixture has a creamy consistency. Add more seasoning, if necessary.

5. Transfer the tofu filling to the pastry case and arrange the tomatoes on top. (If you like, you can drizzle a little olive oil over the tomatoes so that they stay nice and juicy, and brush the edges with a little vegan cream or soya milk.)

Continued on the next page ▶

For the topping (optional)

basil

vegan parmesan (p. 18)

6. Bake the quiche for around 40–50 minutes until the filling is no longer runny and the crust is lightly browned. (If the top starts to get too dark in the oven, loosely cover the quiche with a piece of foil or baking paper.)

7. Leave the quiche to cool for approx. 10 minutes before slicing, and serve sprinkled with vegan parmesan, fresh basil or any other toppings of your choice.

Tips and variations

- You can substitute the plain flour or spelt flour with exactly the same quantity of gluten-free flour mix. If using gluten-free flour, I recommend adding a 'flax egg' to help the dough stay together (combine 1 tbsp. ground flax seeds with 3 tbsp. hot water and leave to stand for 5 minutes).
- For a crispier shortcrust, cover the pastry case with dried beans or chickpeas (so that it doesn't collapse while baking) and blind-bake at 200°C (390°F) for approx. 10 minutes before adding the filling. Once you've blind-baked the pastry, reduce the temperature to 180°C (350°F), remove the beans, add the filling and bake for approx. 30 minutes. You'll find a step-by-step guide to blind-baking shortcrust on p. 19.
- Baking times can vary depending on the quality of the oven, how big the tin is and what it's made of, and whether or not the quiche is covered while baking. I recommend that you check it occasionally to see how the top is looking.

Stuffed spaghetti squash

55 mins
Makes 2 portions

1 spaghetti squash
2 tbsp. olive oil
3 garlic cloves
200 g (7 oz) spinach
    (fresh or frozen)
150 g (5 oz) vegan cream
    cheese (or cashew nut
    sour cream, p. 10)
salt and pepper
150 g (5 oz) vegan feta
    (p. 14)
75 g (⅓ cup) vegan
    parmesan, grated (p. 18)

To garnish (optional)
pine nuts
fresh thyme

1. Preheat the oven to 200°C (390°F).

2. Using a sharp knife, cut the spaghetti squash in half lengthways. Scoop out the seeds with a spoon.

3. Rub 1 tbsp. oil over the insides of the squash and place in a baking tin or on a baking tray with the skin side up. Bake the squash for approx. 40 minutes until the flesh is tender and a fork goes in easily.

4. Leave the squash to cool briefly. Carefully break up the flesh with a fork so that you're left with thin strands that look a bit like spaghetti.

5. Heat 1 tbsp. oil in a pan, roughly chop the garlic and fry for a minute, stirring continuously, until fragrant. Add the spinach and sauté for another minute until it is wilted. Drain any excess moisture from the spinach and then stir in the vegan cream cheese (or cashew nut sour cream). Season with salt and pepper.

6. Divide the creamy spinach mixture between the two halves – or 'boats' – of the squash and stir it in. Arrange the vegan feta on top and sprinkle with a little vegan parmesan.

7. Bake the stuffed boats at 180°C (350°F) for 8–10 minutes. Then turn the oven to the grill or fan setting and bake for another 3–5 minutes until the boats are hot and the cheesy topping is golden brown.

8. For the best results, serve straight from the oven with toasted pine nuts and fresh thyme.

Stuffed peppers with couscous

35 mins
Makes 3–4 portions

4 red peppers
1–2 tbsp. olive oil for frying
    (+ a little extra to brush
    the peppers)
salt and pepper
150 g (5 oz) couscous
300 ml (1⅓ cups) vegetable stock
    (or as stated on the couscous
    packet)
300 g (10 oz) mushrooms
1 large onion
2 garlic cloves
small bunch of parsley
    (+ extra to garnish)
4 handfuls of spinach
1 tin of chickpeas or beans
    (rinsed and drained)
150 g (5 oz) vegan cheese, grated
approx. 4 tbsp. pine nuts

1. Preheat the oven to 180°C (350°F). Cut the top off each pepper (keeping the stem intact), remove the seeds and wash.

2. Brush the inside and outside of the peppers with a little olive oil, then place them into a greased oven-proof dish with the openings pointing upwards. Sprinkle with a little salt and pepper. Roast in the middle of the oven for 8–10 minutes.

3. While the peppers are roasting, pour approx. 300 ml (1⅓ cups) – or the volume stated in the instructions on the packet – of hot vegetable stock over the couscous, cover and leave to stand for approx. 8 minutes, stirring frequently, until the couscous has fully absorbed the stock.

4. Clean and finely chop the mushrooms. Peel and finely dice the onions and chop the garlic and parsley.

5. Heat 1 tbsp. oil in a large frying pan and sauté the onion for 2–3 minutes until translucent. Add the mushrooms and, if necessary, a little more oil and fry for another 4 minutes. Then add the garlic and spinach and fry for another minute until the spinach has wilted.

6. Finally, stir in the chickpeas, couscous, chopped parsley and most of the vegan cheese. Season to taste with a little salt and pepper.

7. Remove the peppers from the oven and fill with the couscous and vegetable mixture. Sprinkle the rest of the vegan cheese on top and grill in the oven for 5–10 minutes.

8. While you're waiting, toast the pine nuts in a small dry pan.

9. Sprinkle the stuffed peppers with pine nuts and fresh parsley, and serve with tzatziki (p. 157) or another dip of your choice.

Soups, stews and curries

Mexican-style bean chilli

35 mins
Makes 4 portions

250 g (9 oz) rice
1 onion
2 garlic cloves
1 red pepper
2 carrots
2 tbsp. olive oil
2 tbsp. tomato purée
2 tsp. ground paprika
1 tsp. cumin
400 g (14 oz) chopped tomatoes
2 tins of beans (e.g. kidney
   beans or black beans), rinsed
   and drained
1 tin of sweetcorn, rinsed
   and drained
300 ml (1¼ cups) vegetable stock
salt and pepper
chilli, to taste

1. Cook the rice according to the packet instructions.

2. While the rice is cooking, peel and finely chop the onion and garlic. Halve the pepper, remove the seeds, wash and finely dice. Peel and finely dice the carrots.

3. Heat the olive oil in a large saucepan and fry the onion, pepper and carrots over a medium heat for around 5 minutes. Add the garlic and sauté for another minute. Add the tomato purée, paprika and cumin and sweat for a short time.

4. Add the tomatoes, beans and sweetcorn. Pour over the vegetable stock and simmer for 15–20 minutes over a low heat.

5. Season with salt, pepper and chilli, and serve with the rice.

Peanut curry with sweet potatoes

30 mins
Makes 4 portions

2 tbsp. olive oil
1 onion, finely chopped
2 garlic cloves, chopped
thumb-sized piece of ginger,
    grated
½ tsp. turmeric
2 tbsp. Thai red curry paste
200 ml (1 cup) passata
2 tbsp. peanut butter
½ tin of coconut milk
    (200 ml/1 cup)
approx. ½ tsp. salt, to taste
juice of ½ lime
1–2 tbsp. coconut sugar
    (or another sugar/syrup)
1 large sweet potato, peeled
    and diced
1 tin of chickpeas, rinsed and
    drained (optional)

For the topping (optional)
fresh parsley or fresh coriander
roasted peanuts

1. Heat the oil in a large saucepan or frying pan. Add the chopped onion and fry for 2–3 minutes, stirring occasionally, until translucent. Add the garlic and ginger, and continue to fry for a minute. Then add the turmeric and curry paste, and sweat for a short time.

2. Add the passata and approx. 480 ml (2 cups) of water and bring to the boil. Stir in the peanut butter and coconut milk. Season with salt, lime juice and coconut sugar.

3. Add the diced sweet potato to the sauce, cover the pan and leave to simmer for 15 minutes.

4. If using, add the tin of chickpeas and warm everything through for another minute.

5. Serve the curry with rice and garnish with parsley or coriander and peanuts.

Creamy mushroom soup

20 mins

Makes 4 portions

2 tbsp. olive oil (or vegan butter,
   coconut milk or canola oil)
1 large onion, diced
750 g (1 lb 10 oz) mushrooms,
   sliced
1 carrot, finely diced
4 garlic cloves, chopped
approx. 2 tsp. fresh thyme,
   to taste
2 tbsp. soy sauce (or tamari,
   gluten-free)
480 ml (2 cups) vegetable stock
2 tbsp. cornflour (or arrowroot
   powder/tapioca flour)
400 ml (1¾ cups) coconut milk
   (or any other plant milk/vegan
   cream)
4 tbsp. vegan parmesan (p. 18) or
   nutritional yeast flakes
sea salt
black pepper
fresh parsley (optional, to garnish)

1. Heat the oil in a large casserole dish or stock pot over a medium heat. Fry the onions for 2–3 minutes until translucent, then add the mushrooms and fry for around 4–5 minutes.

2. Add the carrot, garlic and thyme (and, if necessary, a little more oil) and continue to fry for about 3 minutes until the mushrooms are caramelised. Then deglaze with the soy sauce and give the pan a shake so that the mushrooms are nicely coated. (If you like, you can set aside a large spoonful of the fried mushrooms to garnish the soup later.)

3. In a small measuring jug, mix approx. 5 tbsp. of the vegetable stock with the cornflour. Then add to the mushrooms along with the rest of the vegetable stock and simmer for 1–2 minutes, stirring continuously, until the soup has thickened.

4. If you would like the soup to have a creamier consistency, you can blend the mushroom and stock mixture at this point.

5. Finally add the coconut milk and vegan parmesan, season to taste with salt and pepper and simmer for another 5–10 minutes, stirring occasionally, until the soup is nice and creamy. (Adjust the seasoning, if required, and if the soup is too thick, simply add more stock.)

6. Serve the soup with the mushrooms you set aside, fresh parsley and crusty garlic bread or any other sides you fancy.

Continued on the
next page ▶

For the garlic bread
3–4 tbsp. olive oil
2 garlic cloves, crushed
pinch of salt
4–6 slices of baguette
fresh herbs (optional)

Garlic bread

1. You can bake the bread while the soup is cooking. First, preheat the oven to 200°C (350°F).

2. Mix together the olive oil, garlic and salt in a small cup. Lay the slices of bread on a baking tray and brush with the garlic oil. Bake for around 10–12 minutes or until the bread is crisp and golden. (The baking time will vary depending on the type of bread you use and the thickness of the slices.)

Tips and variations

- **Mushrooms:** Rather than the usual chestnut and button mushrooms, you could try using some different types of mushrooms (e.g. wild mushrooms) or a mixture of different varieties.
- **Coconut milk:** As an alternative to coconut milk, you can also use other plant milks with a high fat content, such as almond or cashew milk. If you're using a more low-fat milk, I recommend replacing some of the milk with vegan cream or adding 2–3 tbsp. almond or cashew butter for a creamier soup. To make a nut-free version, you can use either oat milk or soya milk/cream and either sunflower seed butter or tahini.
- You can either serve the soup chunky or purée it for a creamy consistency. Use a stick blender directly in the pan or transfer the soup to a blender and purée until creamy.
- **Bread:** I use a crusty baguette for the garlic bread but you can also make your own naan bread (p. 151).

Lentil balls in Indian-style curry sauce

45 mins
Makes 4 portions

200 g (7 oz) red lentils
   (or 600 g (1 lb 5 oz)
   pre-cooked lentils)
1 tbsp. olive oil + a little
   extra for brushing
1 large onion, diced
3 garlic cloves, chopped
1 tbsp. tomato purée
2 tsp. curry powder,
   to taste
1 tbsp. soy sauce
   (or tamari)
small bunch of coriander,
   chopped
small bunch of parsley,
   chopped
approx. ¾ tsp. salt, to taste
½ tsp. black pepper (or to
   taste)
4 tbsp. breadcrumbs or
   (gluten-free) oat flour

1. Cook the lentils in a pan of water according to the packet instructions.

2. Preheat the oven to 175°C (350°F) and line a baking tray with baking paper.

3. Heat the oil in a frying pan over a medium heat and fry the diced onion for approx. 2–3 minutes. Add the chopped garlic and sweat for another minute.

4. Place the lentils, onions, garlic, tomato purée, curry powder, soy sauce, coriander, parsley, salt and pepper in a food processor and blend to form a coarse mixture rather than a smooth purée. (You can also combine the ingredients in a bowl and mash with a fork.)

5. Work the breadcrumbs into the lentil mixture, add more seasoning, if required, and leave to stand for 10 minutes. (You can also leave the mixture in the fridge overnight.) Once it has been standing for a while, the mixture should be soft but able to hold its shape once moulded. If it's too sticky, add more breadcrumbs or oat flour.

6. With wet hands, shape the lentil mixture into balls and lay on the baking tray. Brush the balls with a little oil and bake for approx. 30 minutes. Turn after 15–20 minutes.

Continued on the next page ▶

For the curry sauce

1 tbsp. coconut oil

1 onion, chopped

½ red pepper, finely chopped (optional)

3–4 garlic cloves, chopped

1 tsp. fresh ginger, grated

1–2 tsp. cumin

2 tsp. garam masala (or curry powder)

3 large ripe tomatoes, diced (approx. 450 g (16 oz)), or tinned chopped tomatoes/ passata

120 ml (½ cup) water (or more to thin out the sauce)

240 ml (1 cup) coconut milk (or any other plant milk/cream)

approx. 1 tsp. salt, to taste

1 tbsp. coconut sugar (or standard white sugar, to taste)

½ tsp. chilli, to taste

To serve (optional)

rice or naan bread (p. 151)

coconut yoghurt (or vegan cream)

sesame seeds

fresh coriander or parsley

limes

7. While the lentil balls are in the oven, cook the rice (if using) and the curry sauce.

8. Heat the oil in a large frying pan over a medium heat. Add the onion and pepper (if using) and fry for approx. 3–4 minutes. Then add the chopped garlic, grated ginger, cumin and garam masala, and sweat for another minute. Add the tomatoes, water, coconut milk, salt, sugar and chilli. Mix everything together and bring to the boil. Then reduce the heat, cover and leave the sauce to simmer for around 10–15 minutes.

9. Transfer the sauce to a blender and purée until creamy (you can also use a stick blender). Return the sauce to the pan and simmer for another 1–2 minutes. Season to taste and, if it's too thick, add more water.

10. Remove the crispy baked lentil balls from the oven and place in the sauce. Garnish with coconut yoghurt, sesame seeds and fresh coriander. Serve right away with rice or naan bread and a wedge of lime.

Tips and variations

- I recommend you use full-fat coconut milk or a creamy plant milk/vegan cream with a high fat content. You can use low-fat milk with a high water content, but the sauce won't be as creamy.
- For gluten-free lentil balls, you can use gluten-free oat flour. To make your own oat flour, simply blend gluten-free oats to form a flour. Alternatively, you can also use a gluten-free flour mixture or almond flour.
- Any leftover curry sauce or lentil balls are best stored separately in the fridge. If kept in the sauce, the balls will go mushy quite quickly. Re-heat the leftover lentil balls by giving them a quick blast in the microwave, or bake them in the oven to make them crispy again.

Creamy pumpkin and chickpea minestrone

30 mins
Makes 4 portions

1½ tbsp. olive oil
1 large onion, diced
3 carrots, finely diced
4 garlic cloves, chopped
960 ml (4 cups) vegetable stock
240 ml (1 cup) coconut milk (tinned)
2 bay leaves
parsley, oregano and thyme, to taste
approx. 1 tsp. salt, to taste
pepper
2 tbsp. nutritional yeast flakes
170 g (6 oz) lasagne sheets
  (or another type of pasta)
½ head of cauliflower (optional)
1 tin of pumpkin purée (425 g/15 oz)
120 ml (½ cup) tomato passata
1 tin of chickpeas , rinsed and
  drained

To garnish
vegan parmesan (p. 18)
your choice of fresh herbs

1. Heat the oil in a large saucepan and fry the onion over a medium heat for approx. 3–4 minutes. Add the carrots and garlic, and fry for another minute.

2. Add the vegetable stock, coconut milk, bay leaves, herbs, salt, pepper and yeast flakes. Mix everything together and bring the soup to the boil.

3. Break the lasagne sheets into smaller pieces, then add them to the soup and cook for approx. 8–10 minutes (or as per the packet instructions) until al dente. Break the cauliflower into florets and add to the pan once the pasta has been cooking for 5 minutes.

4. Just before the end of the cooking time, remove the bay leaves, add the pumpkin purée, tomato passata and chickpeas, stir well and simmer for another 2–3 minutes. Give the soup a little taste and add more seasoning, if required.

5. Garnish with vegan parmesan and fresh herbs, and serve right away.

Tips and variations
- **How to store:** The soup will become thicker over time, as the pasta soaks up the liquid. However, it will keep in the fridge for up to 4 days if covered. Simply add a little more vegetable stock when you come to reheat the soup later.
- **Coconut milk:** Rather than coconut milk, you could instead use 200 g (1 cup) cashew nut sour cream (p. 10), plus an extra 40 ml (3 tbsp.) water to thin it down.
- **Pumpkin:** You can buy ready-made pumpkin purée in a tin in most supermarkets. However, it's also super quick to make it yourself. Simply cut 450 g of Hokkaido squash (with the skin) or butternut squash (without the skin) into small cubes and cook in a little water for approx. 10 minutes until soft. Then drain off the water, let it stand briefly so that any excess water evaporates, and blend to a purée. Rather than pumpkin or squash, you could also use one large sweet potato.

Creamy tomato soup with cheese toasties

Tomato soup

20 mins
Makes 3–4 portions

900 g (2 lbs) chopped tomatoes
  (fresh or tinned)
1 tbsp. olive oil for frying
1 onion, chopped
3–4 garlic cloves, chopped
120 ml (½ cup) vegetable stock
1 tbsp. tomato purée (optional)
1 tsp. ground paprika (optional)
salt and pepper
80 ml (⅓ cup) coconut milk or
  vegan cream (optional)

To garnish (optional)
coconut yoghurt (or any other
  type of vegan yoghurt)
vegan parmesan (p. 18)
fresh basil

1. If you're using fresh tomatoes, start by peeling and dicing them.

2. Heat the oil in a frying pan or non-stick saucepan over a medium heat. Once the pan's hot enough, add the onions and fry for approx. 4–5 minutes until lightly browned. Add the garlic and fry for another minute, stirring continuously.

3. Pour in the tomatoes and vegetable stock and bring to the boil. Then reduce the heat and simmer for around 8–10 minutes. (If you're using whole tomatoes, carefully crush them with the back of a wooden spoon.)

4. Remove the pan from the heat and season to taste with the tomato purée, paprika, salt and pepper. Transfer the tomato soup into a blender and blend until creamy. Alternatively, you can blend the soup in the pan using a stick blender (just watch out for the mixture splattering).

5. Pour the soup back into the pan, which should still be warm, and finish it off by stirring in the coconut milk or vegan cream.

Continued on the next page ▶

6. Serve the tomato soup in bowls with a dollop of coconut yoghurt, a sprinkling of vegan parmesan and fresh basil, and crunchy toast or a cheese toastie for dunking.

Tips and variations

- If you make the soup with fresh tomatoes, you will need to peel and chop them beforehand, as shown in these photos.
- Because the tomatoes splash so easily, I recommend using a blender that has a lid to purée the soup. If you prefer to use a stick blender to purée the soup directly in the pan, cover the pan with a piece of foil or baking paper, making a hole in the middle for the blender.
- The tomato soup keeps really well in the fridge for up to 4 days and you can reheat it on the hob or in the microwave. It also freezes well.

Vegan cheese toasties

15 mins
Makes 4 toasties

1 tsp. olive oil for frying
1–2 garlic cloves, chopped
3 handfuls of fresh spinach
(or 2 spring onions)
pinch of salt (or more to
taste)
2 tbsp. vegan cream cheese
4 slices of bread (of your
choice)
1 tbsp. vegan butter (or oil)
125 g (4½ oz) vegan
cheddar-style cheese,
grated

1. Heat the oil in a frying pan and fry the garlic for about 30 seconds. Then add the spinach and a pinch of salt and sauté for another minute until the spinach is wilted. Transfer to a bowl and squeeze out any excess moisture. Add the vegan cream cheese and another pinch of salt, to taste, and give it a good stir.

2. Clean the pan (or use another large frying pan) and place over a medium heat.

3. Spread one side of each slice of bread with a little vegan butter. Once the pan is hot enough, add two slices of the bread buttered side down. Sprinkle a little grated 'cheddar' onto each slice. Spoon the spinach and cream cheese mixture on top and sprinkle with a little more 'cheddar' (approx. 60 g/½ cup per toastie). Then place the remaining two slices of bread on top.

4. Press down lightly on the toasties using a turner or spatula. This will help to melt the cheese and make the toastie hold together better. Once the bread on the bottom of the toastie has browned, turn it over and fry the other side until golden brown and crispy (approx. 2–4 minutes on each side).

Continued on the
next page ▶

Tips and variations

- If you'd like the cheesy filling even gooier, heat it in the microwave for another 15–20 seconds after frying.
- Frozen spinach works fine; you just need to defrost it first. Then squeeze out any excess water and mix it with the fried garlic and vegan cream cheese.
- Rather than shop-bought vegan cream cheese, you can also use your own homemade cashew nut sour cream (p. 10) for the creamy spinach mixture.
- Homemade vegan mozzarella (p. 17) also works really well as an alternative to shop-bought vegan cheddar-style cheese.

Coconut curry soup

40 mins
Makes 4 portions

6–7 small potatoes, cut into
   quarters (with the skin left on)
2 tbsp. coconut oil (or canola oil/
   stir-fry oil)
1 onion, thinly sliced
thumb-sized piece of ginger,
   chopped
1–2 carrots, finely diced
1 red pepper, sliced
1 head of broccoli, cut into florets
3 tbsp. red curry paste
2 tins of coconut milk
   (400 ml/1¾ cups each)
4 tbsp. soy sauce
2 tsp. chilli paste (sambal oelek)
1 tsp. rice wine vinegar
1 cup of frozen peas, defrosted
2–3 handfuls of fresh spinach
   (optional)
250 g (9 oz) tofu, cut into cubes

For the topping (optional)
handful of cashews
fresh parsley (or coriander)
2–3 tsp. sesame seeds

1. Boil the potatoes for approx. 8–10 minutes until they have started to soften but are still quite firm. Drain and set aside.

2. While the potatoes are boiling, heat 1 tbsp. oil in a large stock pot. Fry the onion and ginger over a high heat for approx. 2–3 minutes until the onion is translucent. Then add the carrots, pepper and broccoli florets, and fry for a further 2–3 minutes. Add the curry paste and sweat for another minute.

3. Next, add the coconut milk and mix everything together. Add the soy sauce and chilli paste and bring to the boil. Then add the potatoes to the soup and simmer for 5 minutes. Finally, stir in the rice wine vinegar, peas and spinach (if using). Season again.

4. Heat the rest of the oil in a frying pan and fry the tofu until golden brown on all sides. Remove from the pan and then fry the cashew nuts briefly in the same pan.

5. Serve the soup garnished with the tofu, cashews, herbs and sesame seeds.

Top tip
I like to leave the skin on the potatoes for this recipe. However, you can peel them beforehand if you prefer.

Cauliflower soup

25 mins
Makes 4 portions

2 tbsp. oil (of your choice)
1 onion, chopped
4 garlic cloves, chopped
1 head of cauliflower, cut
   into florets
2 small potatoes, peeled
   and diced
480 ml (2 cups) vegetable stock
240 ml (1 cup) plant milk
   (unsweetened)
½ tsp. salt, to taste
pepper, to taste
pinch of nutmeg (optional)
2 tbsp. nutritional yeast flakes,
   to taste

To garnish (optional)
2–3 tbsp. pumpkin seeds and
   sunflower seeds
fresh parsley, chopped

1. Heat 1 tbsp. oil in a large saucepan. Add the onion and fry for around 5 minutes until soft and caramelised. Add the garlic and fry for 30 seconds.

2. Add three quarters of the cauliflower (setting the other quarter aside for the topping), along with the potatoes, vegetable stock and plant milk, and bring to the boil. Then reduce the heat, place the lid on the pan and simmer for around 15–20 minutes or until the vegetables are soft.

3. While that's simmering, heat the remaining oil in a frying pan. Cut the rest of the cauliflower florets into thin slices and sauté them in the hot oil, stirring occasionally, until they have softened and browned.

4. Once the cauliflower and potatoes are cooked, add your seasoning and blend until creamy using a stick blender. (Add more seasoning, if necessary, plus a little more plant milk if the soup is too thick.)

5. Dish the cauliflower soup into bowls. Garnish with the sautéed cauliflower, pumpkin seeds, sunflower seeds, fresh parsley and any other toppings you like.

Tips and variations
- **Plant milk:** I like to use full-fat coconut milk from a tin as it makes the soup deliciously thick and creamy, but you can use any other unsweetened plant milk, or even vegan cream for extra richness.
- The cauliflower soup will keep in the fridge for up to 4 days and freezes well too. When you're ready to eat it, simply warm it up on the hob or in the microwave.

Snacks, sides and healthy fast food

Pizza pockets with samosa-style filling

1 hour + 1 hour to prove
Makes approx. 16 pockets
(depending on size)

For the dough (you can also use shop-bought pizza dough)
25 g (2 tbsp.) fresh yeast
    (or 1 sachet of dried
    yeast)
200 ml (1 cup) lukewarm
    soya milk (or water)
1 tsp. sugar
350 g (2¾ cups) flour
1 tsp. salt
a little vegetable oil
    (to grease the bowl)

Start by making your own yeast dough (see tips on p. 20).

1. Crumble the fresh yeast into the lukewarm soya milk (or water) (alternatively you can use dried yeast). Add the sugar and give everything a good stir. Set aside for around 5 minutes until it starts to foam.

2. Combine the flour and salt in a mixing bowl. Add the yeast mixture and knead well using your hands, or a food processor with the dough hook attachment, until the mixture forms a smooth dough. (If necessary, add a little more water or flour.)

3. Shape the dough into a ball and place in a lightly greased bowl. Cover the bowl with a damp tea towel and leave to prove in a warm place for around 45 minutes to 1 hour, until the dough has doubled in size.

Continued on the next page ▶

For the filling

2 medium potatoes
  (or a mixture of potatoes
  and sweet potatoes)
salt
80 g (½ cup) frozen peas
60 g (⅓ cup) frozen sweetcorn
  (or more peas)
1 onion
1 carrot
2 garlic cloves
1 tbsp. coconut oil for frying
1 tbsp. curry powder
¼ tsp. cayenne pepper
1 tsp. ground coriander
½ tsp. turmeric
¼ tsp. cumin
¼ tsp. ground paprika
3 tbsp. coconut milk

To glaze (optional)

approx. 4 tbsp. soya cream
pinch of turmeric (optional,
  for a yellow colour)

Indian samosa-style filling

1. To make the filling, first peel and dice the potatoes and boil them in salted water for approx. 15 minutes. Add the peas and sweetcorn for the last couple of minutes to defrost them. Then drain off the water and leave the vegetables to stand so that any excess moisture evaporates.

2. Finely dice the onion. Grate the carrot. Chop the garlic. Heat a little oil in a large frying pan and fry the onion for 2–3 minutes until translucent. Add the carrot, garlic and spices, and continue to fry for another minute. Next add the potatoes, peas and sweetcorn, fry for a little while longer and then deglaze the pan with the coconut milk. Set aside and leave to cool.

3. Preheat the oven to 200°C (390°F).

4. Roll the dough out to a thickness of approx. 3 mm (¼ inch) and cut out large discs (approx. 10 cm/4 inch diameter) using a round glass or biscuit cutter.

5. Spoon around 2 tsp. of the filling into the centre of each disc. Then fold one side over the filling to form a semi-circle. Press down the edges a little with your fingers, then use a fork to crimp them. Repeat this step for all the discs.

6. Place the pizza pockets onto a baking tray lined with baking paper, brush with a mixture of soya cream and turmeric (optional) and bake for around 20 minutes until golden.

Tips and variations

- You can also make the dough without yeast but it won't rise quite as well and won't be quite as soft. To do this, simply combine all the other ingredients and knead for 10 minutes to form a smooth dough. Then wrap the ball of dough in cling film and leave to rest for 30 minutes.
- For more advice on making yeast dough, go to page 20.

Vegan naan bread with garlic butter

1 hour 10 mins
Makes 6 naans

120 ml (½ cup) warm
    water
3½ g (1 tsp.) dried yeast
1 tsp. sugar
1 tbsp. olive oil + a little
    extra for frying
60 g (¼ cup) soya yoghurt
½ tsp. salt
300 g (2⅓ cups) plain flour
    (or spelt flour)

**For the garlic butter,
to serve (optional)**
2 tbsp. vegan butter at
    room temperature
    (or coconut oil)
1–2 garlic cloves, finely
    chopped or crushed
salt and pepper
fresh herbs, chopped
sesame seeds

1. Combine the water, yeast and sugar in a large bowl. Set aside for around 10 minutes until the mixture starts to foam.

2. Add the olive oil, soya yoghurt, salt and flour. Mix everything together with a wooden spoon or a fork. Then turn out onto a lightly floured work surface and knead with your hands for 5–10 minutes to form a smooth, soft dough. (Alternatively, you can use a food processor with the dough hook attachment.)

3. Transfer the dough to a lightly greased bowl. Cover with a moist tea towel or cling film and leave to prove in a warm place for around an hour, until the dough has doubled in size.

4. Once proved, divide the dough into 6 pieces. Roll out each piece into a round or oval shape about 5 mm (¼ inch) thick on a lightly floured work surface.

Continued on the next page ▶

5. Heat a cast-iron or non-stick frying pan over a medium heat and brush with a little oil. Fry each naan bread for around 2–3 minutes until bubbles form and the edges look slightly dry. Then turn and fry for another 2–3 minutes on the other side until golden brown. (While you're frying the rest of the naans, I recommend covering the cooked ones with a clean tea towel to keep them warm and soft until you're ready to serve.)

6. Place the vegan butter on a plate. Add the garlic and season to taste with salt, pepper and fresh herbs. Mash to a paste with a fork.

7. Brush the freshly baked naan breads with the vegan garlic butter, or serve plain if you prefer. Sprinkle with sesame seeds and fresh herbs such as thyme, coriander or parsley.

Tips and variations

- You can use whichever type of unsweetened (vegan) natural yoghurt you prefer. Alternatively, you can substitute the yoghurt for vegan cream or coconut cream. For coconut cream, leave a tin of full-fat coconut milk in the fridge overnight. The next day, scoop out the solid creamy part that has formed on the top (this is the coconut cream). If you don't follow a vegan diet, you can also use Greek yoghurt made from cow's milk.
- For more advice on making yeast dough, go to page 20.

Courgette and chickpea burg

25 mins
Makes 2 portions
(3–4 larger burgers or 8 small
fritters)

2 potatoes (approx. 150 g/5 oz
   cooked weight)
2 medium-sized courgettes
1 tin of chickpeas
1 onion
2 garlic cloves
1 tsp. olive oil + 2 tbsp. for frying
approx. 50 g (⅓ cup) chickpea
   flour
½ tsp. cumin
½ tsp. ground coriander
pinch of chilli powder
salt and pepper
100 g (3½ oz) broccoli florets
   (optional)
breadcrumbs to coat (optional)

1. Cook the potatoes, with the skins on, until soft. Then drain off the water, allow them to stand briefly and peel. Set aside and leave to cool.

2. Grate the courgette, add a generous pinch of salt and leave to stand for 5 minutes. Then squeeze out as much excess moisture as possible.

3. Rinse and drain the chickpeas, then coarsely blend in a food processor or blender (you can also use a stick blender).

4. Peel and finely chop the onion and garlic. Heat around 1 tsp. oil in a frying pan and sweat the finely chopped onion for 2–3 minutes until translucent. Add the garlic and fry for a few seconds longer. Set aside and leave to cool.

5. Mash the potatoes with a fork on a large deep plate and then transfer to a large bowl. Add the courgette, chickpeas, onion, garlic, chickpea flour, spices, salt and pepper. Mix well and leave to stand for approx. 5–10 minutes so that the flour soaks up any excess moisture. (If necessary, add a little more flour.) If using, rinse the broccoli florets, pat dry, grate and stir into the mixture.

6. Shape the courgette mixture into whatever size you prefer – you could make larger patties for burgers or smaller ones for dipping. For a crispier coating, you can also roll the patties in breadcrumbs before frying.

Continued on the
next page ▶

For the burger buns

3 tbsp. pine nuts
1 tbsp. olive oil for frying
125 g (4½ oz) mushrooms
1 small courgette
salt and pepper
2 burger buns or bread rolls
a handful of baby spinach
cashew nut sour cream (p. 10)
   (or vegan cream cheese)

7. Heat the oil in a large frying pan over a medium heat and fry the burgers for approx. 3–5 minutes on each side until golden brown.

8. Serve the burgers in buns or enjoy them on their own with your favourite dip.

Assembling your burger buns

1. Toast the pine nuts in a dry frying pan. Remove from the pan and set aside.

2. Add the oil to the pan and heat. Slice the mushrooms and courgette, and fry in the hot oil for approx. 5 minutes. Season with salt and pepper.

3. Slice the burger buns in half and pile them up with fresh spinach, cashew nut sour cream, the courgette and chickpea patties, courgettes, mushrooms and pine nuts. Bon appétit!

Tips and variations
- The burgers should be crunchy on the outside and soft on the inside. If you like them crispier, simply make the patties smaller and thinner.
- As an alternative to chickpea flour, semolina works well. (If you use a different type of flour, you may need to adjust the quantity because not all types of flour absorb the same quantity of liquid.)
- Any leftover patties can be reheated in the oven later. Simply bake for approx. 10 minutes at 180°C (350°F) until they're warm and crispy on the outside.

Barbecue jackfruit burgers with crispy fries

Burger

20 mins
Makes 4 burgers

2 tins of jackfruit in brine
   or water (not in syrup)
1 tsp. ground paprika
2 tsp. ground cumin
   (optional)
1 tsp. dried oregano
   (optional)
1 tsp. ground coriander
   (optional)
½ tsp. salt
1 tbsp. olive oil (or another
   type of oil) + a little
   extra for frying
1 medium-sized onion,
   finely chopped
2 garlic cloves, chopped
1 jalapeño, finely chopped
   with seeds removed
   (optional)
1 cup of barbecue sauce +
   a little extra to serve

1. Drain the jackfruit, rinse thoroughly and pat dry.
Then place in a bowl and shred using your fingers or
two forks. Add the spices, salt and 1 tbsp. oil and mix
well. Leave to marinate for 5 minutes.

2. Heat a little oil in a large frying pan and fry the
onion for approx. 5 minutes. Add the garlic and
jalapeño, if using. Fry for a minute longer until the
garlic is fragrant.

3. Add the jackfruit and fry for approx. 3 minutes,
stirring occasionally, until it is nicely browned and
slightly crispy.

4. Add the barbecue sauce, mix well, cover the
pan and simmer over a low heat for another
10 minutes or until the mixture has the desired
consistency. (If necessary, add a little water while it's
cooking. The longer you cook it for, the softer the
jackfruit will be.)

5. Grate the cucumber with the skin on. Add a good
pinch of salt and set aside for 5–10 minutes.

Continued on the
next page ▶

For the tzatziki
1 cucumber, grated
sea salt
250 g (1 cup) soya yoghurt
2 garlic cloves, chopped
1 tbsp. lemon juice
1 tbsp. olive oil
pepper

To serve (optional)
4 burger buns
salad and vegetables
  (of your choice)
fries (p. 160)

6. Give the cucumber a good squeeze and pour away the salty liquid. Add the soya yoghurt, garlic, lemon juice, olive oil and a little pepper and mix well. Give it another taste and add more salt, garlic, lemon juice or herbs, if needed.

7. Divide the jackfruit mixture between the burger buns. Then pile the buns up with salad, vegan tzatziki or any other veggies you fancy, plus an extra dollop of barbecue sauce. The burgers also taste great with a side of fries (p. 160).

Tips and variations
- There's no need to remove the core and seeds of the jackfruit – they taste just as good as the rest.
- You can use any type of barbecue sauce you like.
- Any leftover jackfruit will keep in the fridge for up to a week and reheats really well.
- The vegan tzatziki will keep in the fridge for up to 5 days depending on the type of yoghurt you use.

Fries

40 mins

Makes 4 portions

1 kg (2 lbs) potatoes
1–2 tbsp. cornflour (or rice flour)
3 tbsp. olive oil
salt
your preferred seasoning
  (e.g. ground paprika)

To serve (optional)
guacamole (p. 168)
ketchup

1. Preheat the oven to 220°C (430°F) with the baking tray inside.

2. Peel the potatoes and cut into sticks around 1 cm (½ inch) thick. (To save time, I like to use a vegetable cutter, but a sharp knife will work just as well.)

3. Rinse the sticks well under running water and then soak them in a bowl of fresh water for approx. 10 minutes to wash away any excess starch.

4. Thoroughly pat the potatoes dry with a clean tea towel or kitchen paper.

5. Then mix with the cornflour, oil and seasoning.

6. Line the pre-heated baking tray with baking paper, spread the fries on top and bake for approx. 25–30 minutes until golden and crispy. Turn after 10–15 minutes.

7. As soon as the fries are crisp and golden, serve right away with guacamole, ketchup or any other dips you fancy!

Top tip
You can also make the fries in an air fryer, if you have one.

Indian-style stuffed flatbreads (aloo paratha)

30 mins + time to stand
Makes 4 flatbreads

For the flatbread
300 g (2⅓ cups) plain flour
   (or spelt flour)
1 tsp. salt
1 tbsp. olive oil
150 ml (⅔ cup) water

For the potato filling
2 medium potatoes
2 tbsp. olive oil for frying
3 spring onions (approx.
   100 g/3½ oz), thinly
   sliced
small bunch of parsley
   (or coriander, approx.
   30 g/¾ cup), chopped
1/3 tsp. garam masala
   (optional)
½ tsp. salt (or to taste)
approx. ½ tsp. black pepper,
   to taste

To serve (optional)
tzatziki (p. 157)

Flatbread dough
1. Combine the flour and salt in a large mixing bowl. Add the oil and water and mix using a chopstick or a fork, until all the water has combined well with the flour.

2. Knead the mixture with your hands until the clumps of flour stick together. (If the dough is still very dry, even after kneading for a while, add an extra 1–2 tbsp. water). Transfer the dough to a work surface and continue to knead until it's smooth and stretchy (approx. 3–5 minutes).

3. Shape the dough into a ball, wrap it in cling film (or cover with a tea towel) and leave to stand for 20–30 minutes.

Potato filling
1. Boil the potatoes, with their the skins on, until soft. Alternatively, prick the potatoes in several places with a fork and cook in the microwave for approx. 10 minutes. (The cooking time will vary depending on the size of the potatoes. You'll know they're ready when you can easily slide a knife into them.)

2. Once the potatoes have cooled down, peel them. Transfer to a bowl and mash coarsely with a fork.

Continued on the next page ▶

3. Heat 1 tbsp. oil in a frying pan and sweat the spring onions for 1–2 minutes to soften them.

4. Add the spring onions and parsley to the potatoes. Season with garam masala, salt and pepper. Give everything a good mix and season again if needed.

Stuffing the flatbreads

1. Divide the dough into four equally sized pieces and shape into balls.

2. Take one ball (cover the rest of the dough so that it doesn't dry out) and, using a rolling pin, roll it out on a lightly floured work surface to form a 20–22 cm (8 inch) disc. Spread a quarter of the filling onto one half of the disc, leaving a 1–1.5 cm (½ inch) gap around the edge.

3. Moisten the edge with a little water, fold the other side of the dough over the filling and press down firmly.

4. Repeat this process with the remaining pieces of dough.

Baking the flatbreads

1. Heat the rest of the oil in a large cast-iron or non-stick frying pan over a medium heat.

2. Place one or two stuffed flatbreads into the pan and fry until golden brown, pressing the edges down lightly with a turner or spatula so that the flatbreads are evenly browned. Then turn over and fry on the other side.

3. Once cooked, place the flatbreads on a cooling rack so that they stay crispy.

4. Serve the flatbreads with vegan tzatziki or any other dip you like.

Top tip

If you want to use spelt flour or wholemeal flour, you will need to adjust the quantity of water, because different types of flour have different levels of absorbency. Start with the quantity of water specified in the recipe and then add 1 extra tbsp. at a time until you have the right consistency. When it's ready, the dough should be smooth and stretchy and not sticky or crumbly.

Spring rolls

45 mins
Makes 20

small chunk of red cabbage
small chunk of white
    cabbage
125 g (4½ oz) smoked tofu
1 large carrot
3 spring onions
salt
1 tbsp. cornflour (or flour) +
    1–2 tbsp. water to seal the
    pastry
20 frozen spring
    roll pastry sheets
    (approx. 275 g/10 oz),
    21.5 x 21.5 cm (8.5'' x 8.5'')
vegetable oil for frying/
    brushing

For the sauce
2 tbsp. soy sauce (or tamari,
    gluten-free)
1 tbsp. rice wine vinegar
½ tbsp. sesame oil
2 tsp. agave syrup
½ tsp. ginger, finely grated
pinch of chilli flakes
    (optional)

To serve (optional)
1 tbsp. sesame seeds
1 tbsp. spring onions, finely
    chopped

1. Thinly slice the red and white cabbage using a mandolin. Pat the tofu dry and peel the carrot. Then cut both into thin strips. Finely chop the spring onions.

2. Add a little salt to the cabbage and mix with your hands for approx. 2–3 minutes to soften it. Then leave it to stand for around 10 minutes before squeezing out any excess moisture.

3. In a small dish, mix the cornflour with a little water.

4. Place one of the spring roll pastry sheets onto a work surface or chopping board, with one corner pointing towards you. (Cover the rest of the sheets with a damp tea towel so that they don't dry out.)

5. Place a small pile of the vegetables and tofu onto the lower part of the pastry sheet.

6. Next, roll the pastry up tightly. Stop rolling halfway and fold in the outer corners.

7. Brush a little of the cornflour paste onto the upper corner (so that it's ready to stick to the roll). Then continue to roll up the spring roll. Once finished, place each of the spring rolls under a damp tea towel or a piece of cling film so that they don't dry out.

Continued on the next page ▶

8. Pour the oil into a saucepan so that it's approx. 5–8 cm (2–3 inches) deep and heat to 185°C (365°F). (It you dip the end of a wooden chopstick into the oil, it should sizzle.) Carefully place the spring rolls into the oil, one at a time, and fry them in batches (depending on how many you can fit into the pan at once). It's important to make sure you leave enough space between each one. Fry the spring rolls for around 3–5 minutes or until they're golden brown, carefully turning them in the oil using a chopstick, so that they fry evenly on each side. Once cooked, place the spring rolls on a piece of kitchen paper to soak up any excess oil.

9. Mix together all the ingredients for the sauce in a small bowl.

10. Garnish the spring rolls with sesame seeds and freshly chopped spring onions, to taste, and serve alongside the sauce while they're still hot and crispy.

Tips and variations

- You can also bake the spring rolls in the oven, if you prefer. To do this, brush the spring rolls with a little oil and lay on a baking tray lined with baking paper. Bake in a preheated oven at 220°C (430°F) for around 30 minutes or until they're crisp and golden, turning halfway through.
- If you use other vegetables with a high water content, make sure you squeeze out as much of the moisture as you can, or sauté the vegetables first to steam off some of the water. Otherwise, the delicate pastry sheets will go soggy and tear.
- The spring rolls freeze really well. Simply lay them on a lightly floured tray, leaving a little space between each one, and freeze for 2–3 hours. Once they're frozen, you can transfer them to a sealable freezer bag.

Sweet potato wedges with guacamole

35 mins
Makes 2 portions

1 large sweet potato
2 tbsp. vegetable oil
1 tsp. ground paprika
1 tsp. coarse sea salt

For the guacamole
1 avocado
1 garlic clove, crushed
2 tsp. lemon juice
salt and pepper

1. Preheat the oven to 200°C (390°F) and line a baking tray with baking paper.

2. Wash the sweet potato and pat dry. Cut off the ends of the sweet potato, cut it in half, then into quarters and then again into wedges, leaving the skins on.

3. Mix the wedges with the oil, paprika and salt in a large bowl and then spread over a baking tray. Bake for approx. 20–25 minutes, turning after 15 minutes. (The smaller and thinner the wedges are, the less time they will take to cook. Chunkier wedges will take a little longer.)

4. For the guacamole, start by halving the avocado and removing the stone. Scoop out the flesh with a spoon and then mash with a fork. Drizzle over the lemon juice and add the crushed garlic. Season to taste with salt and pepper.

5. Serve the sweet potato wedges with the guacamole and enjoy!

Sweet potato quesadillas

20 mins
Makes 4 portions

1–2 tbsp. olive oil + 3 tsp.
1 sweet potato (approx.
  250 g/9 oz), grated
1 tsp. ground paprika
½ tsp. chilli (optional)
½ tsp. cumin (optional)
handful of baby spinach
1 tin of black beans, rinsed
  and drained
½ tin of sweetcorn, rinsed
  and drained
2–3 tbsp. fresh parsley,
  chopped
salt and pepper
6 (gluten-free) tortillas
  (approx. 20 cm/8 inch
  diameter)
approx. 150 g (5 oz) vegan
  cheese, grated
guacamole (p. 168) to
  serve (optional)

1. Heat the oil in a large frying pan. Add the sweet potato and fry for approx. 30 seconds. Add the spices and mix well.

2. Add a little water, cover the pan and turn down the heat to make sure nothing burns. Leave to simmer for around 6 minutes, stirring occasionally.

3. Add the baby spinach, stir and simmer for another 2 minutes, until the sweet potato is tender and cooked through.

4. Stir in the beans, sweetcorn and parsley, and warm everything through for another minute. Season with salt and pepper.

5. Heat a non-stick frying pan over a medium heat and brush with the rest of the oil.

6. Place a tortilla in the pan and spread around 3 tbsp. of the filling evenly over one half, leaving a narrow gap around the edge. Cover the filling with grated cheese and fold the other half of the tortilla over the filling (to 'close' it). Press down lightly with a turner or spatula so that the two halves stick together.

7. Fry the tortilla for approx. 2–3 minutes, then carefully turn it over and fry on the other side until crisp and golden.

Continued on the next page ▶

8. Repeat this process with the rest of the filling and as many tortillas as you need to use it all up (approx. 4–6, depending on the size).

9. Place the cooked tortillas on a chopping board and use a sharp knife or pizza cutter to slice them into three pieces.

10. Serve warm with guacamole or any other dips of your choice, and enjoy!

Top tip

Any leftover tortillas can be wrapped in cling film and kept in the fridge. Before serving, simply reheat them in the microwave or oven.

Sweet treats and desserts

Austrian-style shredded pancake with plum compote 178

Mango mousse 181

Peanut butter cups with caramel sauce 185

Creamy vanilla parfait 187

Apple hand pies 189

Chocolate mousse torte 191

Gingerbread biscuits 195

Coconut bites 199

Pistachio ice cream 200

Austrian-style shredded pancake with plum compote

15 mins

Makes 2 portions

150 g (1¼ cups) plain flour
   or spelt flour
1 tbsp. baking powder
30 g (2½ tbsp.) sugar (or maple
   syrup)
300 ml (1⅓ cups) soya milk
100 ml (½ cup) mineral water
1 tbsp. lemon juice
dash of vanilla extract (optional)
2–3 tbsp. raisins (optional)
2 tbsp. vegan butter
   (or margarine)
60 ml (5 tbsp.) grape juice (or
   vegan red wine + 1–2 tbsp.
   sugar)
250 g (9 oz) plums, pitted
1 tsp. cornflour

For the topping (optional)
icing sugar
redcurrants
flaked almonds

1. Place the flour, baking powder, sugar, soya milk, water, lemon juice and vanilla in a bowl and whisk to form a smooth batter before stirring in the raisins.

2. Heat the vegan butter in a large, non-stick frying pan. Pour in the batter and fry for 3–4 minutes over a medium heat. Using two turners or spatulas, turn the pancake over and fry on the other side for another 2–3 minutes. Use a turner or spatula to break the pancake into bite-sized pieces and fry for another 2–3 minutes until golden.

3. Bring the grape juice to the boil in a saucepan. Cut the plums into quarters, add to the pan and simmer over a low heat for approx. 5 minutes.

4. Mix the cornflour with 2–3 tbsp. water in a cup to form a smooth paste and stir in with the plums, continuing to simmer. Once the compote has thickened, remove the pan from the heat.

5. Serve the shredded pancake with the warm plum compote. If you like, you can also dust the pancake with icing sugar and decorate with redcurrants and flaked almonds.

Mango mousse

10 mins + time to cool
Makes 6 glasses

1 large mango, peeled and
with the stone removed
200 g (7 oz) soya quark
1–2 tbsp. sugar or syrup
(to taste)
200 ml (1½ cups) non-
dairy whipping cream
1 tsp. agar (enough for
500 ml (2 cups) liquid)
80 ml (⅓ cup) plant milk
(or water)

To decorate (optional)
blackberries
desiccated coconut

1. Purée the flesh of the mango using a blender or
stick blender. Add the soya quark and sugar (or syrup)
and mix well until creamy.

2. In a separate high-sided mixing bowl, whip the
cream with an electric hand whisk.

3. Add the plant milk (or water) to a small saucepan
and stir in the agar until it has fully dissolved. Bring
to the boil, continuing to stir, and then simmer for
approx. 2 minutes (or for the time specified on the
packet).

4. Remove from the heat and quickly combine the
agar mixture with the creamy mango. Then fold in the
whipped cream right away. Only mix for as long as
is needed to combine the ingredients; otherwise the
whipped cream will collapse.

5. Spoon the mango mousse straight into glasses and
leave to set in the fridge for at least an hour. Then
decorate with blackberries or desiccated coconut and
enjoy chilled!

Continued on the
next page ▶

Tips and variations

- **Soya quark:** If you can't get hold of soya quark, you can use vegan yoghurt instead, or you can blend silken tofu to a creamy purée and use that.
- **Vegan cream:** As an alternative to non-dairy whipping cream, you can use pure coconut cream instead. To make your own, simply leave a tin of full-fat coconut milk in the fridge overnight. The next day, scoop the solid coconut cream from the top of the tin and save the runny coconut water for another recipe.
- **Agar:** Different products contain different quantities of agar, so please check the list of ingredients to make sure the product contains 100% agar. Otherwise you will need to adjust the quantity according to the packet instructions. You need enough for 500 ml (2 cups) of liquid.

Peanut butter cups with caramel sauce

15 mins + time to cool
Makes 6 large cups
(or 20 mini cups)

200 g (7 oz) vegan
  chocolate
100 g (½ cup) peanut
  butter
2 tbsp. icing sugar

**For the topping
(optional)**
roasted peanuts
coarse sea salt

For the caramel sauce
150 ml (⅔ cup) coconut
  milk (tinned)
150 g (¾ cup) sugar

1. Line a muffin tray with paper cases.

2. Roughly chop the chocolate, place in a heat-proof bowl and melt gently over a pan of simmering water, stirring occasionally.

3. Spoon approx. 1 tbsp. of the melted chocolate into each paper case so that it covers the base. Place the tin in the freezer for around 10–15 minutes to allow the chocolate to set.

4. While you're waiting, mix the peanut butter with the icing sugar to form a creamy paste and transfer to a piping bag.

5. Take the muffin tray out of the freezer and pipe a little of the peanut mixture into the centre of each case, leaving a little space around the edges.

6. Spoon the rest of the melted chocolate on top so that the peanut butter is completely covered. Sprinkle the tops with the roasted peanuts and sea salt. Then place in the freezer for another 15 minutes.

Caramel sauce

1. Combine the sugar and coconut milk in a saucepan and bring to the boil. Allow to simmer, stirring occasionally, until the mixture has a caramel-like consistency.

2. Transfer the sauce to a clean jar and leave to cool. Drizzle over the cups and save the rest in an air-tight jar in the fridge to enjoy another day!

Creamy vanilla parfait

10 mins + time to cool
Makes 3–4 portions

500 ml (2 cups) plant milk
35 g (2 tbsp.) cornflour
1 tsp. vanilla extract
3–4 tbsp. sugar (or syrup),
  to taste
120 ml (½ cup) non-dairy
  whipping cream

For the topping (optional):
raspberries
pomegranate seeds
desiccated coconut

Top tip
I like to use non-dairy
whipping cream, but if you
can't get hold of any you
can use coconut cream
instead. To make your own,
simply leave a tin of full-fat
coconut milk in the fridge
overnight, then scoop out
the solid coconut cream
from the top of the tin and
save the coconut water for
a different recipe.

1. Take approx. 5 tbsp. of the plant milk and mix it with the sugar, vanilla extract and cornflour in a cup.

2. Pour the rest of the plant milk into a saucepan and bring to the boil. Stir in the cornflour mixture and bring back to the boil, stirring continuously. (You may wish to add a little extra sweetener or vanilla extract, according to taste.)

3. Once the custard has thickened, remove from the heat and allow to cool a little, stirring occasionally. Pour into a bowl and seal tightly with cling film (so that the custard doesn't form a skin). Leave the custard to cool at room temperature, then transfer to the fridge until chilled.

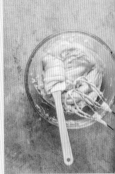

4. Remove the custard from the fridge and take off the cling film.

5. In a mixing bowl or jug, beat the non-dairy whipping cream with an electric hand whisk until it forms stiff peaks. Then set aside and mix the custard until it is nice and creamy. (There's no need to wash the whisk attachment between each use.) Then carefully fold the whipped cream into the custard using a spatula or whisk.

6. Divide the parfait mixture into glasses and enjoy straight away or keep in the fridge until you're ready to serve.

7. Garnish with fresh raspberries, pomegranate seeds, desiccated coconut or other fruit.

Apple hand pies

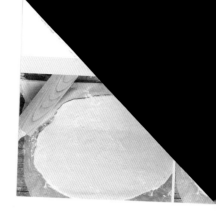

30 mins + time to cool

Makes 12 hand pies

For the pastry:
300 g (2⅓ cups) plain flour
   or spelt flour
2 tbsp. sugar
1 tsp. salt
180 g (¾ cup) cold vegan butter,
   cut into cubes
75 ml (5 tbsp.) cold water

For the apple and cinnamon filling:
2 apples
75 ml (5 tbsp.) water
1 tsp. cornflour
3 tbsp. brown sugar
1 tsp. cinnamon
dash of vanilla extract
dash of lemon juice (optional)

To glaze:
plant milk/cream
brown sugar

Shortcrust pastry:
1. Combine the flour, salt and sugar in a large bowl. Add the cubes of butter and rub them into the flour using your fingertips. Gradually add the cold water and knead just long enough to form a dough.

2. Transfer the dough to a floured work surface and shape into a ball. Wrap in cling film and place in the fridge for least 30 minutes.

Filling:
1. Peel the apples, remove the cores and chop into small cubes.

2. Combine the water, cornflour, sugar, cinnamon, vanilla extract and lemon juice in a saucepan. Bring to the boil, stirring continuously until the mixture thickens.

3. Add the apples, mix well and set aside.

Assembling the hand pies:
1. Preheat the oven to 180°C (350°F).

2. Roll out the pastry on a lightly floured work surface.

3. Cut out discs using a circular item such as a glass or a large cookie cutter.

4. Shape any leftover dough into a ball, roll it back out and cut out more discs. (Alternatively, you could also cut the leftover pastry into different shapes and use it to bake biscuits.)

5. Spoon approx. 1 heaped tbsp. of the apple filling into the centre of half the discs. Moisten the edge of each disc with a little water to help them stick together.

Continued on the next page ▶

6. Place the remaining pastry discs over the filled discs and carefully press down the edges with a fork to seal the pies.

7. Brush the top of the pies with a little plant milk or cream, and cut two slits in the top so that the steam can escape while they're baking. You may also wish to sprinkle them with a little brown sugar.

8. Bake the pies for approx. 20 minutes until golden brown.

9. Allow to cool for around 10 minutes before serving.

Top tip
The pies will keep in a sealed container at room temperature for up to 2 days, or 3–4 days in the fridge.

Chocolate mousse torte

15 mins + time to cool
Ingredients to fill a
23/24 cm (9 inch) tart tin

28 Oreo cookies
(320 g/11 oz) or other
biscuits
80 g (⅓ cup) vegan butter,
melted

For the chocolate mousse
225 g (8 oz) vegan dark
chocolate, chopped
480 ml (2 cups) non-dairy
whipping cream

For the chocolate ganache
170 g (6 oz) vegan dark
chocolate, chopped
180 ml (¾ cup) non-dairy
whipping cream

For the topping (optional):
fresh fruit (e.g. figs,
blackberries and
blueberries)
desiccated coconut

1. Place the whole Oreo cookies in a food processor or blender and blitz into fine crumbs. (Alternatively, you can put the cookies into a freezer bag and crush them with a rolling pin.)

2. Transfer the crumbs to a bowl, add the melted butter and combine well.

3. Press the buttery biscuit mixture into a tart tin (or pie tin/springform tin) with a removable base. Leave to set in the fridge or freezer for 15 minutes. (For a crunchier biscuit base, you can pre-bake it in the oven for 10 minutes).

Chocolate mousse
1. Place the chopped chocolate in a heat-proof dish. Heat 150 ml (⅔ cup) of the whipping cream in a small saucepan. As soon as it begins to boil, remove from the heat and pour over the chocolate. Wait a little, then stir until smooth and leave to cool to around room temperature.

2. In a high-sided mixing bowl or jug, beat the rest of the whipping cream with an electric hand whisk until it's just starting to form stiff peaks. Then carefully fold in the chocolate and cream mixture. Only stir for as long as necessary; otherwise the whipped cream will collapse. Spoon the mixture onto the prepared biscuit base right away, and smooth over the top. Leave the torte to set for approx. 4 hours (or overnight) in the fridge.

Continued on the next page ▶

Chocolate ganache

1. Place the chopped chocolate in a heat-proof dish. Heat the whipping cream in a small saucepan. As soon as it begins to boil, remove from the heat and pour over the chocolate. Wait a little, then stir until smooth and leave to cool to room temperature. Spread the ganache over the top of the chocolate mousse and return the torte to the fridge for another 30 minutes.

2. Garnish with fresh fruit, desiccated coconut or any other toppings you like. Serve chilled and enjoy!

Tips and variations

- This recipe also works with gluten-free sandwich biscuits. Likewise, you can use biscuits without a creamy filling, such as 250 g (9 oz) vegan shortbread (or gluten-free equivalent). To make up for the lack of filling in the biscuits, just add an extra 55 g (¼ cup) vegan butter.
- If you'd like the biscuit base a little crunchier, blind-bake it in the oven at 175°C (350°F) for around 10 minutes. Allow to cool completely before adding the mousse filling; otherwise the mousse will melt.
- Rather than non-dairy whipping cream, you can use a different type of vegan cream or coconut cream and coconut milk (full-fat). For the mousse, you will need 120 ml (½ cup) coconut milk to melt the chocolate and 360 ml (1½ cups) coconut cream for whipping. For the ganache, you can mix together 60 ml (5 tbsp.) coconut milk and 120 ml (½ cup) coconut cream and bring to the boil.
- To make your own coconut cream, simply leave 2–3 tins of full-fat coconut milk in the fridge overnight. The next day, scoop out the solid part that has set at the top of the tin, then whip it as you would with cream.

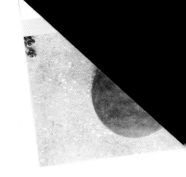

Gingerbread biscuits

30 mins + time to cool
Makes 12 large or 24 small
biscuits

1 flax egg (or 4 tbsp. smooth
   apple sauce/apple purée)
250 g (2 cups) plain or spelt flour
   (or a gluten-free flour mix)
1 tsp. bicarbonate of soda
   (or 2 tsp. baking powder)
¼ tsp. salt
2 tsp. ground ginger
2 tsp. ground cinnamon
¼ tsp. ground nutmeg
45 g (3 tbsp.) vegan butter,
   at room temperature
100 g (½ cup) coconut sugar
   (or brown sugar)
80 g (¼ cup) molasses (or golden
   syrup)

1. To make the flax egg, stir 1 tbsp. of ground flax seeds (or chia seeds) into 3 tbsp. hot water in a small cup. Leave to stand for 5 minutes.

2. Combine the flour, bicarbonate of soda, salt, ginger, cinnamon and nutmeg in a bowl.

3. In a separate bowl, cream together the vegan butter and coconut sugar. Add the molasses and flax egg, and mix until everything is well combined.

4. Gradually add the flour mixture and stir with a wooden spoon to form a sticky dough. (If the dough is too sticky, add a little extra flour.) Divide the dough into two portions and shape each into a ball, flattening them down a little. Tightly wrap the balls of dough in cling film and place in the fridge for at least an hour.

5. Once the dough has chilled, pre-heat the oven to 175°C (350°F) and dust a work surface with a generous amount of flour.

6. Using a lightly floured rolling pin, roll out the dough to a thickness of around 5 mm (¼ inch). Dust your preferred cookie cutter with flour and cut the dough into shapes. With the help of a pallet knife or spatula, carefully transfer the biscuits to a baking tray lined with baking paper. Leave a gap of approx. 5 cm (2 inches) between each one. Roll out any leftover dough once again and cut out more shapes. Repeat this step with the second ball of dough.

Continued on the next page ▶

7. Bake the gingerbread biscuits for 8–10 minutes or until they're crisp and golden on the outside.

8. Leave the biscuits to cool on the tray for 5 minutes (during which time they will also start to firm up). Then transfer them to a cooling rack and allow to cool completely.

9. Before serving, dust the biscuits with icing sugar or decorate as you wish.

Top tip
The biscuits will keep for several days at room temperature.

Coconut bites

15 mins + time to cool
Makes 20

35 g (2½ tbsp.) coconut oil
65 g (2½ oz) creamed
    coconut
20 g (2 tbsp.) almond
    butter (or cashew butter)
25 g (2 tbsp.) maple syrup
    (or rice/agave syrup)
20 g (4½ tbsp.) desiccated
    coconut (+ extra to
    coat)
20 blanched almonds

1. Place the coconut oil, creamed coconut and almond butter (or cashew butter) in a heat-proof bowl and melt over a pan of simmering water (or in the microwave), until the ingredients are well combined.

2. Stir in the maple syrup and desiccated coconut and leave the mixture cool in the fridge for 30 minutes (or 10 minutes in the freezer), until it has started to set.

3. Once the mixture is solid enough, shape it into 20 little balls using your hands and press an almond into the centre of each one. Then coat each ball with desiccated coconut.

4. The coconut bites will keep in the fridge for up to a week and can also be frozen.

Pistachio ice cream

10 mins + time to cool
Makes enough to fill a 20 cm
(8 inch) loaf tin

200 g (7 oz) pistachios, shelled
250 g (1 cup) vegan cream
100 ml (½ cup) water
juice of ½ lemon
80 g (3½ tbsp.) maple syrup
   (or another syrup)
¼ tsp. salt
dash of vanilla extract

1. Toast the pistachios in a dry pan. Then leave to cool.

2. Blend the pistachios with the rest of the ingredients until smooth and creamy.

3. Transfer the creamy pistachio mixture to a loaf tin and place in the freezer. Give it a stir every 30 minutes until the ice cream has set.

Top tip
Of course, you can also use an ice cream maker if you have one.

Cakes and muffins

Blueberry custard tart with a crumble topping

1 hour 5 mins + time to cool
Makes enough for one 22 cm
(9 inch) tart tin

For the shortcrust pastry
240 g (just under 2 cups) plain or
  spelt flour + 60 g (½ cup) for
  the crumble topping
100 g (½ cup) coconut sugar
  (or white sugar)
¼ tsp. salt
170 g (¾ cup) vegan butter,
  chilled
3–4 tbsp. cold plant milk

For the custard filling
400 ml (1¾ cups) coconut milk
75 ml (5 tbsp.) almond milk
55 g (3½ tbsp.) cornflour
1 tsp. vanilla extract
60 g (⅓ cup) sugar
100 ml (½ cup) vegan cream

For the topping
300 g (2 cups) fresh blueberries
  (please don't use frozen
  berries!)
handful of flaked almonds
2 tsp. brown sugar (optional)

Shortcrust pastry
1. Combine the flour, sugar and salt in a large mixing bowl.

2. Cut the vegan butter into small cubes and add to the flour mixture, along with the plant milk. Quickly knead the mixture with your hands to form a dough. Shape the dough into a ball, flatten slightly and wrap in cling film. Chill in the fridge for around half an hour.

Custard filling
1. Pour the coconut milk into a saucepan and bring to the boil. While you're waiting, combine the almond milk, cornflour and vanilla extract in a small cup. Then stir the mixture into the hot coconut milk along with the sugar, bring back to the boil and allow to simmer for a short time, stirring continuously, until the custard is thick and creamy.

2. Once it's cooked, transfer the custard to a bowl, seal tightly with cling film and leave to cool to room temperature. (This method is the same as for the creamy vanilla parfait, for which there are step-by-step photos on p. 187.)

Continued on the
next page ▶

Tips and variations

- **Gluten-free pastry:** You can substitute the flour for exactly the same quantity of gluten-free flour mix. If using gluten-free flour, I recommend adding a 'flax egg' to help the dough stay together (combine 1 tbsp. ground flax seeds with 3 tbsp. hot water and leave to stand for 5 minutes).
- **Coconut milk and almond milk:** You can also use any other type of plant-based milk or cream, or a flavoured creamy drink. If you use a sweetened product, use less syrup/sugar.
- **How to store:** The tart will keep for up to 4 days in the fridge.

Assembling the tart

1. Once the pastry dough has chilled, pre-heat the oven to 180°C (350°F) and lightly grease a tart tin or springform tin.

2. Take around three quarters of the dough and roll it out on a floured work surface to form a circular disc that's slightly larger than the tin. Carefully transfer the dough to the tart tin and press it firmly into the base and sides. Prick the pastry base in several places using a fork.

3. To make the crumble topping, add 60 g (½ cup) of flour to the remaining pastry dough and knead until crumbly.

4. In a narrow measuring jug with high sides, whip the vegan cream using an electric hand whisk.

5. Remove the cling film from the chilled custard and blend until creamy using the hand whisk. (There's no need to wash the whisk attachment between uses.) Then fold in the whipped cream, spoon the mixture into the pastry case and smooth over the top.

6. Sprinkle about half of the blueberries on top, along with the cobbler mixture and flaked almonds. For more of a glazed finish, you can also sprinkle over some brown sugar.

7. Place the tart in the pre-heated oven and bake for approx. 45 minutes, until the cobbler topping is wonderfully crisp and golden. (Because of the whipped cream, the filling will rise a little in the oven, but it will sink back down as soon as you open the oven door.)

8. Leave the tart in the tin to cool before serving (or ideally overnight in the fridge, to give the filling time to set fully). Carefully remove it from the tin, decorate with the rest of the blueberries and enjoy!

Cheesecake brownies

55 mins
Makes 16

For the cheesecake mixture
225 g (8 oz) vegan cream cheese
125 g (½ cup) soya yoghurt
40 g (¼ cup) sugar
1 tbsp. cornflour
½ tsp. vanilla extract

For the brownie batter
2 flax eggs (or 100 g (½ cup)
   unsweetened apple purée)
120 g (½ cup) vegan butter
   (or margarine/coconut oil)
120 g (4 oz) vegan dark
   chocolate
½ tsp. vanilla extract
120 g (1 cup) flour (or gluten-
   free flour)
pinch of salt
½ tsp. baking powder
¼ tsp. bicarbonate of soda
150 g (¾ cup) brown sugar
approx. 60 ml (5 tbsp.) plant milk
   (or hot coffee)

Toppings
85 g (3 oz) vegan chocolate chips

1. Preheat the oven to 175°C (350°F). Lightly grease a square 21 cm (8 inch) cake tin (or a similar sized tin) and line with baking paper, leaving a little extra paper to hang over the sides. (This will make it easier to lift the brownies out of the tin. Greasing the tin first helps the baking paper to stick.)

2. Prepare the flax eggs by mixing 2 tbsp. ground flax seeds with 6 tbsp. hot water. Then leave to stand for 5–10 minutes.

3. While you're waiting, place all the ingredients for the cheesecake mixture into a mixing bowl and mix to a creamy consistency using an electric hand mixer.

4. Melt the vegan butter along with the chocolate and vanilla extract in a saucepan.

5. In another bowl, combine the flour, salt, baking powder, bicarbonate of soda and sugar. Add the flax eggs, plant milk and melted butter and chocolate mixture, and mix well to form a smooth, creamy batter.

6. Pour a third of the brownie batter into the prepared cake tin, covering the base. Then add alternate heaped tablespoons of the cheesecake mixture and brownie batter to the tin, creating a sort of marbled effect, until both mixtures have been used up.

Continued on the next page ▶

7. Bake the brownies for around 40 minutes or until they reach your preferred consistency. (The longer you bake the brownies for, the drier they will be. If you like a gooier brownie, don't bake them for too long.)

8. Once baked, leave the brownies to cool. Then carefully lift out of the tin using the excess paper.

9. To slice the brownies, dip a sharp knife into some hot water. Then quickly dry it with a piece of kitchen paper and use the warm knife to cut the brownies into squares.

10. For the best results, warm the brownies up for a few seconds in the microwave before serving. This will make them really gooey and creamy.

Tips and variations

- **Gluten-free:** The brownies also work well with a gluten-free flour mix. Simply use exactly the same quantity as specified for the flour.
- **Egg substitutes:** Rather than flax eggs, you could also use 100 g (½ cup) apple purée or a mashed ripe banana. If you do use fruit, I would recommend adding a little less sugar to the batter as the fruit has a natural sweetness.
- **How to store:** The brownies will keep in a sealed container for up to 5 days in the fridge. You can also freeze them as individual portions. Simply put a small piece of baking paper between each brownie and place them in a sealable freezer bag. This ensures that they don't freeze together, so you can easily take them out one at a time.

Lemon and blueberry muffins

35 mins
Makes 12 muffins

juice of 1 lemon + a little grated zest
2 tbsp. soya yoghurt (or apple purée)
180 ml (¾ cup) plant milk
280 g (2¼ cups) plain or spelt flour (or a gluten-free flour mix)
1 tbsp. cornflour or soya flour
2 tsp. baking powder
1 tsp. bicarbonate of soda
½ tsp. salt
125 g (just over ½ cup) vegan butter (or margarine)
130 g (⅔ cup) sugar
1 tsp. vanilla extract
100 g (⅔ cup) fresh blueberries (or frozen)

1. Preheat the oven to 180°C (350°F). Line a 12-hole muffin tray with paper cases.

2. Squeeze the lemon juice into a measuring jug, then add the soya yoghurt and plant milk (there should be approx. 240 ml (½ pt.) in total). Mix everything together and leave to stand for approx. 10 minutes until the mixture curdles to form a sort of vegan buttermilk.

3. Sieve the flour and cornflour into a large bowl. Add the baking powder, bicarbonate of soda and salt, and mix well.

4. In a separate bowl, use an electric hand whisk to cream together the vegan butter, sugar, vanilla extract and lemon zest.

5. Switch the mixer to a low speed setting. Mix in half the flour mixture, followed by the vegan buttermilk and then the rest of the flour mixture, until you have a nice smooth batter (try not to mix for too long).

6. Carefully fold in the blueberries and divide the batter between the muffin cases.

7. Bake the muffins for about 20–25 minutes until a skewer or cake tester comes out clean.

8. Leave to cool in the tray for 10 minutes, then transfer to a cooling rack and leave to cool completely.

Top tip
If you're using frozen blueberries, it's better not to defrost them beforehand. Simply take them straight out of the freezer and mix them with 1 tbsp. cornflour or plain flour to keep them dry.

Panna cotta tart

45 mins + time to cool
Makes enough for one
22/24 cm (9 inch) tart tin

For the shortcrust pastry
250 g (2 cups) plain or
  spelt flour (or gluten-free
  flour mix)
50 g (¼ cup) sugar
½ tsp. salt
120 g (½ cup) vegan
  butter (chilled and cut
  into small cubes)
5 tbsp. cold water
2 tbsp. vegan cream
  (optional, to brush the
  edges for a better glaze)

For the vegan panna cotta
500 ml (2 cups) coconut
  milk
1 tsp. agar (enough for
  500 ml (2 cups) liquid)
80 ml (5½ tbsp.) agave
  syrup (or another type of
  syrup/sugar)
2 tsp. vanilla extract

For the fruity mirror glaze
240 ml (1 cup) red fruit
  juice (of your choice)
½ tsp. agar

Shortcrust pastry
1. Place the flour, sugar, salt, chilled butter and water into a large bowl and knead with your hands to form a smooth dough (or use a food processor). Roll the dough into a ball, flatten slightly, wrap in cling film and place in the fridge for around half an hour to make it slightly firmer and easier to roll out (p. 10).

2. Once it has chilled, roll out the dough between two layers of cling film (or floured baking paper). Transfer to a tart or quiche tin, ideally with a removable base. Remove the cling film and press the dough evenly into the tin.

3. Wrap the tart tin (now lined with the pastry) in cling film and chill in the fridge for another 30 minutes. (The raw dough will keep in the fridge for up to 5 days and is also fine to freeze).

Blind-baking the pastry
1. Preheat the oven to 200°C (390°F).

2. Prick the base in a few places using a fork. Then line the inside of the pastry case with baking paper and weigh it down with dried rice, beans or chickpeas.

3. Bake the pastry case in the pre-heated oven for 15 minutes, until the edges are lightly browned. Then remove from the oven and carefully take out the baking paper and whatever you used to weigh it down.

Continued on the next page ▶

Place the pastry case back into the oven and bake for another 10–15 minutes until the base is golden brown.

4. Leave the baked pastry case to cool fully.

Vegan panna cotta

1. Pour half the coconut milk into a saucepan. Stir in the agar and boil, stirring continuously, for 2 minutes (or for the time specified on the packet).

2. Remove from the heat, quickly stir in the syrup or sugar, along with the vanilla extract and the rest of the coconut milk, and pour straight into the prepared pastry case. (In theory, you could just add all the ingredients to the pan in one go and then bring to the boil, but in my experience the agar powder doesn't dissolve as well if there's a lot of liquid.)

3. Leave the tart to cool in the fridge for an hour until the top has set.

Fruity mirror glaze

1. Pour the red fruit juice into a pan. Stir in the agar and simmer, stirring continuously, for 2 minutes (or for the time specified on the packet).

2. Leave the mixture to cool a little before pouring it over the panna cotta. Place the tart back in the fridge for another 2 hours.

3. Once the filling has set, you can remove the tart from the tin by carefully pushing up the removable base. Garnish with fresh fruit and enjoy!

Tips and variations
- **Gluten-free:** You can substitute the flour for exactly the same quantity of gluten-free flour mix. If using gluten-free flour, I recommend adding an extra 'flax egg' to help the dough stay together (combine 1 tbsp. ground flax seeds with 3 tbsp. hot water and leave to stand for 5 minutes).
- **Coconut milk:** You can also use any other type of plant-based milk or cream, or a flavoured creamy drink. If you go for a sweetened product, I recommend using less syrup/sugar. The best thing to do is just give it a quick taste.
- **Agar:** Different products contain different quantities of agar, so please check to make sure the product contains 100% agar. Otherwise you will need to adjust the quantity according to the packet instructions. You need enough for 500 ml (2 cups) of liquid.

American-style cheesecake

1 hour + 10 mins
Makes enough for one
20 cm (8 inch) springform
tin

150 g (5 oz) vegan
  shortbread biscuits
75 g (⅓ cup) vegan butter,
  melted

For the filling
850 g (1 lb 14 oz) vegan
  cream cheese
1 tin of coconut cream
  (400 ml/1¾ cups)
200 g (1 cup) sugar
4 tbsp. cornflour
1 tbsp. vanilla extract
juice of ½ lemon

For the strawberry and raspberry coulis
150 g (1 cup) frozen
  raspberries
150 g (1 cup) frozen
  strawberries
approx. 2 tbsp. sugar,
  to taste
2 tbsp. cornflour (mixed
  with 2 tbsp. water)

1. Preheat the oven to 175°C (350°F). Lightly grease a 20 cm (8 inch) springform tin and line the base and sides with baking paper.

2. Place the biscuits in a food processor and blitz to fine crumbs. (Alternatively, put them in a freezer bag, squeeze out the air and seal, and crush with a rolling pin.)

3. Transfer the biscuit crumbs to a bowl and mix together with the melted vegan butter.

4. Spread the buttery biscuit mixture onto the base of the prepared tin and press down firmly. Then set aside while you prepare the filling.

5. In a mixing bowl, beat the vegan cream cheese with an electric hand whisk until smooth and creamy. Then add the coconut cream, sugar, cornflour, vanilla and lemon juice. Blend until the mixture is smooth and creamy, occasionally using a spatula to scrape off any mixture that gets stuck to the sides of the bowl.

6. Spoon the creamy cheesecake mixture onto the biscuit base and spread evenly.

7. Wrap the outside of the tin with a double layer of foil so that the base and sides are well covered and no water can leak in. Lift the wrapped tin into a larger cake tin and pour approx. 4 cm (1½ inches) hot water into the larger tin to create a water bath. Bake in the oven for an hour.

Continued on the next page ▶

8. Switch the oven off, leaving the cheesecake inside to stand for another hour. Then open the oven door and allow the cheesecake to cool to room temperature. (The cheesecake might seem a bit wobbly, but it will set even more once it's in the fridge.)

9. Remove the cheesecake from the water bath, carefully remove the foil and chill in the fridge overnight. It's best not to remove the cheesecake from the tin until the following day.

Strawberry and raspberry coulis

1. Defrost and purée the fruit in a saucepan. Add the sugar and bring to the boil. Mix the cornflour with a little water and stir into the puréed fruit. Bring back to the boil, stirring continuously, and simmer for approx. 1–2 minutes until the mixture has thickened a little. Then leave to cool (the sauce will thicken even more as it cools).

2. Serve the cheesecake with the strawberry and raspberry coulis and enjoy!

Tips and variations
- **Water bath:** The water bath helps the cheesecake to bake through evenly and stops it from cracking. The recipe will still work without a water bath, but it's really quite easy to make one and you will taste the difference.
- **Cream cheese/cream:** It's the combination of cream cheese and cream that gives you that classic American-style creamy cheesecake consistency. You can also swap half the cream cheese for a nice firm soya quark and an extra tbsp. cornflour.
- **Coconut cream:** If you can't find coconut cream in the shops, you can leave 2 cans of full-fat coconut milk in the fridge overnight and then scoop out the solid part that has set on the top. (That's the coconut cream.) Alternatively, another type of vegan cream will do the job, as long as it's fairly thick and creamy.
- **Fresh berries:** If you want to make the coulis with fresh berries, you won't need quite as much cornflour.
- **How to store:** The cheesecake will keep in the fridge for up to 5 days or in the freezer for up to 2 months.

Courgette and chocolate cake

1 hour 10 mins
Makes enough for a 25 cm
(10 inch) loaf tin

160 g (1¼ cups) plain or spelt
  flour (or gluten-free flour mix)
1 tbsp. cornflour
50 g (⅓ cup) cocoa powder
1 tsp. baking powder
1 tsp. bicarbonate of soda
½ tsp. salt
1 ripe banana (or 125 g (½ cup)
  apple purée or 2 flax eggs)
60 ml (5 tbsp.) plant milk
  (e.g. soya milk)
½ tsp. instant coffee powder/
  granules or ¼ tsp. ground
  espresso (optional)
100 ml (½ cup) oil (e.g. canola
  oil, melted coconut oil or vegan
  butter)
150 g (¾ cup) brown sugar
  (or maple syrup, agave syrup
  or coconut sugar)
1 tsp. vanilla extract
1 tsp. apple cider vinegar
250 g (9 oz) courgette, grated
150 g (5 oz) vegan chocolate
  chips (or chopped/melted
  chocolate) + a few extra
  to garnish (optional)
Caramel sauce (p. 185), to serve

1. Preheat the oven to 175°C (350°F). Lightly grease the loaf tin and line with baking paper.

2. Sieve the flour, cornflour, cocoa powder, baking powder, bicarbonate of soda and salt into a large bowl and combine using a whisk.

3. Mash the banana with a fork and transfer to a measuring jug. Pour the plant milk into a microwave-safe cup, warm through in the microwave and then mix in the coffee, if using. Add to the banana along with the oil, sugar, vanilla extract and apple cider vinegar and mix thoroughly.

4. Pour this mixture in with the dry ingredients and mix for no longer than required for everything to be just combined.

5. Squeeze any excess moisture out of the grated courgette and add to the batter along with the chocolate chips. The batter should be relatively thick and creamy, but still pourable, as shown in the step-by-step photos. If necessary, you can add a little more milk.

6. Spoon the batter into the loaf tin and sprinkle a few more chocolate chips over the top (optional). Bake the cake for approx. 50–60 minutes or until a skewer placed into the centre comes out mostly clean – with just a little melted chocolate stuck to it.

Continued on the next page ▶

7. Leave the cake to cool in the tin. Then carefully lift it out using the excess baking paper.

8. Cut the cake into slices. It tastes especially delicious served with caramel sauce!

Tips and variations

- **Flour:** I recommend using plain flour, spelt flour or a mixture of wholemeal and plain flour (which will make the sponge a little denser). If you use oat flour or just wholemeal flour, the cake won't be quite as soft and fluffy as with a lighter flour. If necessary, add more milk, as different types of flour often absorb different amounts of liquid.
- **Egg substitutes:** The puréed banana acts as an egg substitute. If you prefer, you can use 125 g (½ cup) apple purée/unsweetened apple sauce instead, or 2 flax eggs. For the flax eggs, mix 2 tbsp. ground flax seeds with 6 tbsp. warm water. Then set aside for 5 minutes until the mixture thickens.
  (If you're not following a vegan diet, you could also use two hen's eggs instead.)
- **Coffee:** You won't necessarily be able to pick out the coffee flavour, but it will intensify the flavour of the chocolate.
- **Chocolate:** You can either stir the chopped chocolate (or chocolate chips) straight into the batter or melt them in a bowl over a pan of simmering water beforehand, as shown in the step-by-step photos.
- **How to store:** The cake will keep in the freezer for up to 3 months. Simply wrap it in cling film and then put it in a sealable freezer bag to protect it from freezer burn. Leave to defrost overnight in the fridge before serving.
- **Muffins:** This recipe can also be used to make muffins, in which case you reduce the baking time to approx. 25–30 minutes. For a tray bake, bake the batter in a brownie tin for approx. 35 minutes.
- **Skewer test:** To check if the cake is ready, you can stick a skewer into the centre. If it comes out almost clean, with just a bit of melted chocolate on it, it's cooked.

Cranberry crumble loaf

I hour
Makes enough for a 25 cm
(10 inch) loaf tin

For the crumble topping (optional)
40 g (⅓ cup) spelt or plain flour or (gluten-free) oat flour
2 tbsp. brown sugar
½ tsp. cinnamon
45 g (3 tbsp.) vegan butter, chilled and cut into cubes

For the batter
250 g (2 cups) spelt or plain flour (or gluten-free flour)
2 tsp. baking powder
½ tsp. bicarbonate of soda
½ tsp. salt
150 g (¾ cup) coconut sugar (or any other sugar)
240 ml (1 cup) almond milk (or any other plant milk)
80 ml (⅓ cup) melted coconut oil
2 tbsp. almond butter (optional)
1 tsp. vanilla extract
1 tbsp. orange juice (or lemon juice/white wine vinegar)
2 tsp. orange zest
120 g (4 oz) cranberries fresh or frozen

1. Preheat the oven to 180°C (350°F). Lightly grease a loaf tin and line with a strip of baking paper, leaving a little extra paper hanging over each side.

2. To make the crumble, mix together the flour, sugar and cinnamon in a medium-sized bowl. Cut the cold butter into small cubes, add to the flour mixture and knead with your hands to form a crumble mixture. Place in the fridge to use later.

3. For the cake batter, combine the flour, baking powder, bicarbonate of soda, salt and sugar in a large mixing bowl. Then set aside.

4. In a measuring jug, mix together the almond milk, melted coconut oil, almond butter, vanilla extract, orange juice and zest. Then pour the wet mixture in with the dry ingredients. Mix well to form a smooth batter and then fold in the cranberries.

5. Transfer the batter to the prepared cake tin. Sprinkle the crumble mixture evenly over the top and press it down lightly so that it sticks to the batter.

6. Bake the cake for 45–60 minutes. Stick a skewer into the centre of the cake. If it comes out almost clean, the cake is ready.

Continued on the next page ▶

For the orange glaze
60 g (½ cup) icing sugar
1–2 tbsp. orange juice
    (or lemon juice)

7. Once baked, leave the cake to cool in the tin for 10–15 minutes. Then carefully lift it out of the tin using the excess baking paper. Transfer the cake to a cooling rack and let it cool a little longer.

8. In a small measuring jug, mix together the icing sugar and orange juice. Once the cake is cooled, drizzle the glaze over the top. Cut into slices and enjoy!

Tips and variations

- **Flour:** I recommend using spelt or plain flour, or a gluten-free flour mix. If you'd like to try the recipe with different types of flour, you'll need to adjust the quantity of almond milk, as different types of flour have different levels of absorbency. Also, if you use a heavy flour like wholemeal, the cake won't be quite as fluffy. It would work better to use a mixture of light and darker flour.
- **Coconut oil:** Instead of coconut oil, you could use another mild-flavoured oil such as canola oil or melted vegan butter. You can also substitute some of the oil with apple purée.
- **Cranberries:** You can chop the cranberries smaller or leave them out altogether. If you're using frozen cranberries, don't defrost them beforehand. Simply roll them in a little flour or cornflour and then fold them into the batter. Alternatively, you can use 1 cup of dried cranberries.
- **How to store:** The cake will keep at room temperature for a day, in the fridge for up to 5 days, or as long as 5 months in the freezer. To defrost, simply leave it in the fridge overnight and then allow it to come up to room temperature before serving.
- **Muffins:** You can also use this recipe to make around 15 muffins. They will take 25 minutes to bake.

Apricot and coconut cake

1 hour 10 mins + time to cool
Makes enough for one 24 cm (9 inch) springform tin

400 g (14 oz) fresh apricots
260 g (2 cups) plain flour
  (or spelt flour)
2 tsp. baking powder
1 tsp. bicarbonate of soda
⅓ tsp. salt
130 g (⅔ cup) sugar
180 ml (¾ cup) soya milk
  (or any other plant milk)
3 tbsp. soya yoghurt
  (or another type of
  yoghurt or apple purée)
120 ml (½ cup) mild-
  flavoured oil (or vegan
  butter)
2 tbsp. lemon juice
  (or apple cider vinegar)
1 tbsp. lemon zest
  (optional)
2 tsp. vanilla extract
4 tbsp. desiccated coconut
  (optional)

For the topping (optional)
coconut flakes (or
  desiccated coconut/flaked
  almonds)
2 tbsp. brown sugar for
  sprinkling

1. Preheat the oven to 180°C (350°F). Lightly grease the sides of the tin and line the base with baking paper.

2. Halve the apricots and remove the stones. If they're not quite soft and ripe enough, you can cut them into quarters or thin slices instead.

3. In a mixing bowl, combine the flour, baking powder, bicarbonate of soda, salt and sugar using a whisk.

4. Mix together the soya milk, soya yoghurt, oil, lemon juice, lemon zest and vanilla extract in a measuring jug.

5. Then pour the wet mixture in with the dry ingredients and combine to form a smooth batter. (Don't mix it for too long; otherwise the sponge will be too dense.) Finally, fold in the coconut flakes.

6. Pour the batter into the prepared tin and smooth over the top. Arrange the apricots on top, and sprinkle with coconut flakes and a little brown sugar, to taste.

7. Bake the cake for 50–60 minutes or until a skewer inserted into the centre of the cake comes out almost clean (with just a few moist crumbs stuck to it).

8. Leave to cool before serving and enjoy!

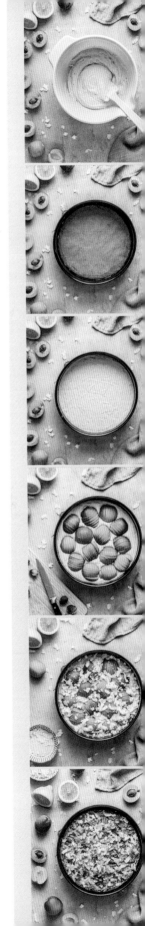

Apple blondies

45 mins
Makes 8

For the spiced apples

2 medium-sized apples,
   peeled and diced
1–2 tbsp. brown sugar
½ tsp. cinnamon

For the batter

200 g (just under 1 cup)
   vegan butter (or
   margarine/melted
   coconut oil)
250 g (2 cups) flour
1½ tsp. baking powder
½ tsp. salt
1 tsp. cinnamon
¼ tsp. nutmeg (optional)
250 g (1¼ cups) brown
   sugar
120 g (½ cup) apple purée
   (or 1 puréed banana
   or 2 flax eggs)
1½ tsp. vanilla extract

1. To make the spiced apple mixture, peel and dice the apples and place them in a bowl. Add the sugar and cinnamon, and mix everything together. (Alternatively, you can cook the diced apples for approx. 3–5 minutes in 2–3 tbsp. water to soften them.)

2. Preheat the oven to 180°C (350°F). Grease a baking tin (28 x 18 cm (11 x 7 inches) or a similar size) with a little vegan butter and line with baking paper, leaving a little excess paper to hang over the sides.

3. To make the batter, cut the butter into slices, transfer it to a frying pan or saucepan and slowly melt it, stirring occasionally. Then set aside to allow it to cool a little.

4. Combine the flour, baking powder, salt, cinnamon, nutmeg and sugar in a bowl using a whisk. Then add the melted butter, apple purée and vanilla extract. Mix it all together to form a thick, sticky batter, then fold in the diced apple.

Continued on the next page ▶

For the topping (optional)
walnuts, chopped
caramel sauce (p. 185)

5. Spoon the batter into the prepared tin and smooth over the top (a lightly greased spatula works well). Bake the blondies for approx. 35 minutes or until the top is golden brown and a skewer comes out almost clean. (The longer you bake the blondies, the drier and crumblier they will be. So don't bake them for too long if you like them moist. If you'd rather make a whole cake instead of blondies, you can bake the batter for a little longer.)

6. Remove the blondies from the oven and leave in the tin until they're almost completely cooled. Then use the excess paper to lift them out of the tin.

7. Before serving, sprinkle with the chopped walnuts and drizzle a little caramel sauce over the top. Cut into small squares and enjoy!

Tips and variations
- **Flour:** I recommend using plain flour, spelt flour or a mixture of wholemeal and plain flour (which will make the sponge a little denser). If you use oat flour or just wholemeal flour, the blondies won't be quite as soft and fluffy as with a lighter flour.
- **Egg substitutes:** As an alternative to apple purée, you can use 1 mashed ripe banana or 2 flax eggs. For the flax eggs, stir 2 tbsp. ground flax seeds into 6 tbsp. hot water and leave to soak for approx. 5 minutes.
- **How to store:** You can cover the blondies and store them at room temperature for up to 2 days, in the fridge for up to 5 days, or in an air-tight container in the freezer for around 3 months. I recommend placing a piece of baking paper between each blondie so that they don't freeze together and you can take them out individually. To defrost them, simply leave in the fridge overnight.
- **Butter/oil:** Since hydrogenated fats like butter and coconut oil solidify in the fridge, the blondies will be harder when chilled. You may therefore want to take them out of the fridge around an hour before serving. Alternatively, you can warm them up in the microwave for a few seconds.

The ultimate chocolate cake

1 hour + time to cool
Makes enough for two
20 cm (8 inch) springform
tins

1 tbsp. apple cider vinegar
   (or lemon juice)
240 ml (1 cup) plant milk
1–2 tsp. instant coffee
   granules (optional)
2 tsp. vanilla extract
240 ml (1 cup) boiling
   water
240 g (just under 2 cups)
   plain flour (or gluten-free
   flour)
120 g (1 cup) cocoa
   powder
300 g (1½ cups) sugar
1 tbsp. baking powder
1 tbsp. bicarbonate of soda
   (or extra baking powder)
1 tsp. salt
180 ml (¾ cup)
   mild-flavoured oil
   (e.g. canola oil)
120 g (½ cup) apple purée
   (or 2 flax eggs)

1. Preheat the oven to 175°C (350°F). Grease two 20 cm (8 inch) springform tins and line the bases with baking paper.

2. Mix the apple cider vinegar with the plant milk and leave to stand for approx. 10 minutes until the mixture curdles to form a sort of vegan buttermilk.

3. Stir the instant coffee and vanilla extract into the hot water.

4. Place the flour, cocoa powder, sugar, baking powder, bicarbonate of soda and salt in a bowl and mix well.

5. Pour the vegan buttermilk, oil and coffee into the dry ingredients. Then add the apple purée and mix the batter with an electric hand whisk on a low setting until the mixture is well combined (but do not over-mix). You can vary the amount of sugar depending on how sweet a tooth you have.

6. Pour the batter into the prepared tins and bake for around 40–45 minutes or until a skewer placed into the centre of the cakes comes out mostly clean, with just a few moist crumbs stuck to it. (The longer you bake the cakes, the drier the sponge will be.) Then leave the cake to cool completely; otherwise the mousse and icing will melt.

7. To make the ganache, bring the cream to the boil in a small saucepan (or heat in the microwave for approx. 2 minutes).

Continued on the next page ▶

For the chocolate ganache
240 ml (1 cup) non-dairy
   whipping cream (or full-
   fat coconut milk)
340 g (12 oz) vegan
   chocolate, chopped
2–3 tbsp. agave syrup (or
   40 g (⅓ cup) icing sugar)

**For the chocolate mousse
(optional)**
80 ml (⅓ cup) non-dairy
   whipping cream (at room
   temperature)
80 ml (⅓ cup) chocolate
   ganache
2 tbsp. icing sugar

8. Pour the cream over the chopped chocolate and stir until the chocolate has melted.

9. Add the agave syrup and mix well.

10. Set 80 ml (⅓ cup) of the ganache aside for the chocolate mousse and leave the rest to chill in the fridge for 2 hours until it's thickened to a spreadable consistency.

11. To make the chocolate mousse, combine the whipping cream with the 80 ml (⅓ cup) of chocolate ganache you put aside earlier, then place in the fridge.

12. Once the mixture has cooled completely, you can whisk it to make a creamier mousse, adding the icing sugar as you go.

13. Place one of the sponges on a serving plate and spread the chocolate mousse on top. Then place the second sponge on top and cover the whole cake, including the sides, with the chocolate ganache.

14. Decorate the cake with whatever fresh fruit you like and enjoy!

Tips and variations
- **Flour:** To make the cake gluten-free, you can use exactly the same quantity of gluten-free flour mix.
- **Egg substitutes:** You can replace the apple purée with 2 flax eggs (simply mix 2 tbsp. ground flax seeds with 6 tbsp. hot water, and leave to soak for 5 minutes).
- **Vegan cream:** I use non-dairy whipping cream for the mousse, but if you can't get hold of any, you can use coconut cream instead – just make sure it can be whipped!
- **Muffins:** If you want to use this recipe to make muffins instead, reduce the baking time to about 25 minutes.

Grams to Cups Conversion Chart

Butter

Cups	Grams	Ounces
¼ cup	57 g	2.01 oz
⅓ cup	76 g	2.68 oz
½ cup	113 g	3.99 oz
1 cup	227 g	8.00 oz

All-Purpose Flour and Confectioners' Sugar

Cups	Grams	Ounces
⅛ cup	16 g	0.563 oz
¼ cup	32 g	1.13 oz
⅓ cup	43 g	1.50 oz
½ cup	64 g	2.25 oz
⅔ cup	85 g	3.00 oz
¾ cup	96 g	3.38 oz
1 cup	128 g	4.50 oz

Granulated Sugar

Cups	Grams	Ounces
2 tbsp.	25 g	0.89 oz
¼ cup	50 g	1.78 oz
⅓ cup	67 g	2.37 oz
½ cup	100 g	3.55 oz
⅔ cup	134 g	4.73 oz
¾ cup	150 g	5.30 oz
1 cup	201 g	7.10 oz

Packed Brown Sugar

Cups	Grams	Ounces
¼ cup	55 g	1.90 oz
⅓ cup	73 g	2.58 oz
½ cup	110 g	3.88 oz
1 cup	220 g	7.75 oz

Index

Contact for questions or suggestions: info@rivaverlag.de

Important note
This book is intended for information purposes. It is not a substitute for a personal medical consultation and should not be used as such. For medical advice, please consult a qualified doctor. The publisher and the author shall not be liable for any negative effects directly or indirectly associated with the information given in this book.

First published in 2020 by **riva Verlag**, part of Münchner Verlagsgruppe GmbH. This English language edition published in 2020 by **Lotus Publishing**, Apple Tree Cottage, Inlands Road, Nutbourne, Chichester, PO18 8RJ, UK

Many thanks to Das Küchenhaus Bielefeld for their support.

Editor: Ulrike Reinen
Cover design: Isabella Dorsch
Cover images: Bianca Zapatka, Sascha Koglin
Images on the inside pages: Bianca Zapatka
Photos: p. 2, 8, 24, 48, 72, 93, 98, 120, 146, 176, 204: Sascha Koglin, Seventysix Media
Layout: Katja Muggli, Medlar Publishing Solutions Pvt Ltd., India
Translation: Surrey Translation Bureau
Printing: Bell & Bain Ltd, UK

British Library Cataloging-in-Publication Data
A CIP record for this book is available from the British Library.
ISBN 978-1-913088-19-4

You can find more information on the publisher at:
lotuspublishing.co.uk